The Lure of Technocracy

The Lure of Technology

Jürgen Habermas

The Lure of
Technocracy

Translated by Ciaran Cronin

polity

First published in German as *Im Sog der Technocratie* © Suhrkamp Verlag Berlin, 2013

This English edition © Polity Press, 2015

The translation of this work was supported by a grant from the Goethe-Institut which is funded by the German Ministry of Foreign Affairs.

Polity Press
65 Bridge Street
Cambridge CB2 1UR, UK

Polity Press
350 Main Street
Malden, MA 02148, USA

ISBN-13: 978-0-7456-8681-3
ISBN-13: 978-0-7456-8682-0 (pb)

A catalogue record for this book is available from the British Library.

Library of Congress Cataloging-in-Publication Data

Habermas, Jürgen.
[Im Sog der Technokratie. English]
The lure of technocracy / Jürgen Habermas.
    pages cm
  ISBN 978-0-7456-8681-3 (hardcover : alk. paper) -- ISBN 0-7456-8681-8 (hardcover
: alk. paper) -- ISBN 978-0-7456-8682-0 (pbk. : alk. paper) -- ISBN 0-7456-8682-6
(pbk. : alk. paper) 1. Jews, German. 2. Jews--Germany. 3. Technocracy. 4. Europe--
Politics and government--1989- 5. Eurozone. 6. Political culture--Europe. I. Title.
  B3258.H323I413 2015
  300--dc23
                          2014035912

Typeset in 11 on 13 Sabon by Servis Filmsetting Ltd, Stockport, Cheshire
Printed and bound in the United Kingdom by T.J. International Ltd, Padstow,
Cornwall

For further information on Polity, visit our website: politybooks.com

Contents

Contents

Preface to the English Edition

The texts included in the third part of this essay collection deal with the relationship between Jews and Germans, a topic that touches the most sensitive nerve of the political self-understanding of citizens of the Federal Republic of Germany. The essay on Heinrich Heine also revisits the European theme of the two preceding parts of the volume.

In the first part, the title essay, which presents my view of the crisis politics of the Eurozone, is followed by two more strictly academic contributions. My interest in the complex issue of European integration has always also been informed by the viewpoint of the philosophy of law. The entirely unique character of the European Union has thus far eluded clear conceptualization in political science and constitutional law. If the project is not destined to fail after all, then this unification process could signal a decisive step towards a postnational world order, one which is also indispensable if unbridled global capitalism is to be steered into socially acceptable channels. The second part of the book contains political interventions from the past two years. They are meant to familiarize British readers in particular with a German perspective on problems that affect us all. In both respects, the present book is a continuation of my two previous studies on European politics.[1]

However, the results of both the most recent European election and current opinion polls reflect a high degree of scepticism towards and rejection of 'Brussels'. Given this desolate state of affairs, my perseverance in advocating European integration will be greeted with amazement. But in view of the deepening European political divide between the continent and the UK, it is all the more necessary for us to familiarize ourselves with each other's perspectives.

The unanimous opposition of all British parties to the election of Jean-Claude Juncker as President of the European Commission, and hence as the leader of the Brussels executive, was a clear signal of the antagonisms that exist – and have existed from the beginning – between the UK and most continental countries over the goal of European unification. To date, conflicts over goals have been sparked mainly by the question of whether each of the incremental territorial 'enlargements' of the Union must be followed by a corresponding 'deepening' of its institutions – or whether the purpose of the Union should be more or less exhausted in a single market.

Since the banking and sovereign debt crisis, the question of further integration has acquired renewed urgency. On this occasion, economic imperatives necessitated another step of integration within an insufficiently institutionalized monetary union – that is, within the Eurozone.[2] In the UK, this development has stirred up old conflicts, even if the *triggering* causes of the increasing Europhobia did not have their origin in the country itself but on the continent.

In order to avert the dangers of the current economic crisis, the member states of the European Monetary Union have been compelled to engage in closer intergovernmental cooperation over the past five years. This has led to regulations that fall far short of halting the trend towards increasing imbalances between the national economies of these countries. However, the new technocratic form of cooperation, which for the present still largely eludes democratic controls, has increased the awareness of an already existing shortfall in legitimacy. The national parliaments have been caught by surprise by the measures to combat the crisis. As a result, there is a heightened sensitivity in the Eurozone that the European decision-making structures are in need of an overhaul. This explains the outrage that arose here when, after the most recent European election, the heads of government wanted to disregard the most successful among the candidates fielded by the European parties for the post of President of the Commission. The need for further democratization is felt more strongly in the core European countries than in the countries on the periphery.

To be sure, these causes are merely triggers for the dispute over the objectives that the citizens associate with European unification. Such conflicts over goals carry weight when they break out, even for understandable reasons, between whole nations. Attitudes towards the project of unification that was once outlined in visionary terms by Winston Churchill are shaped by a mixture of national interests and the historical self-understanding of a nation. Such an issue cannot be a matter of the one side being right and the other wrong. In retrospect, the political elites are at worst open to the charge of having pressed ahead with this project over the heads of their populations. Now, in a long-overdue process of political will-formation among the citizens themselves, lost ground has to be *recuperated* under unfavourable circumstances.

It may help us to gain a better understanding of national differences to recall the truly historic speech delivered by the great statesman and rousing orator Churchill in the Festsaal of the University of Zürich on 19 September 1946.[3] The Shakespearean format of this speech has often been praised. One need only call to mind the ruined landscape of a Europe reduced to rubble and bled to death in the immediate aftermath of the Second World War, the recent mass murders and crimes against humanity, to be amazed even today at the improbability and the visionary power of that far-sighted perspective presented in this speech. To his contemporaries, this man, whom they knew to be an inveterate political realist, must have seemed like a dreamer.

Churchill is clearly aware of this situation and speaks first in the conditional: 'If Europe were once united in sharing of its common inheritance, there would be no limit to happiness, to the prosperity and the glory . . .' Then he evokes present and future dangers – 'the dark horizons for the approach of some new peril, tyranny and terror' – but only to offer a surprising answer to the rhetorical question of what could rescue the situation: 'We must build a kind of United States of Europe.' Given the perplexity that this could be expected to arouse among his audience, he appeals to the courage of the hesitant: 'All that is needed is the resolve of hundreds of millions of men and women to do right instead of wrong and to gain as their reward blessing instead of cursing.' And then Churchill becomes practical, well aware that his proposal could not fail to appear unreasonable to a contemporary audience: 'I am now going to say something that will astonish you. The first step in the re-creation of the European family must be partnership between France and Germany. . . . The structure of the United States of Europe will be such as to make the material strength of a single state less important. Small nations will count as much as large ones . . .' From these beginnings a supranational union of states should progressively emerge: 'Why should there not be a European group which could give a sense of enlarged patriotism and common citizenship to the distracted people of this turbulent and mighty continent?'

It may come as a surprise to *today's* readers that Churchill mentioned the vantage point from which he was speaking only at the end of his address – with his impassioned words, he was appealing as a Briton to Frenchmen and Germans, and to their neighbours. He was addressing those governments and peoples of the continent who would be called the 'core' of Europe only half a century later, from the perspective of a friendly and helpful observer. As was still quite obvious at the time, he saw Great Britain and the Commonwealth, alongside America and Russia, as 'sponsors' of the unification process he was recommending.

Almost seven decades later, the improbable has become a reality. Even the British themselves have in the meantime become citizens of the European Union. And soon they will have to make up their own minds whether they want to withdraw back into the observer perspective of the far-sighted adviser of that time, or whether they prefer after all to remain true to the role that they have adopted in the meantime – that of addressees who followed his wise counsel.

Jürgen Habermas
Starnberg, August 2014

I

The Lure of Technocracy

1

The Lure of Technocracy

A Plea for European Solidarity

(1) In its current form, the European Union owes its existence to the efforts of political elites who were able to count on the passive consent of their more or less indifferent populations as long as the peoples could regard the Union as being also in their economic interests, all things considered. The Union legitimized itself in the eyes of its citizens primarily through the results it produced rather than by fulfilling the citizens' political will. This can be explained not only from the history of its origins but also from the legal constitution of this unique formation. The European Central Bank, the Commission and the European Court of Justice have intervened most profoundly over the decades in the everyday lives of European citizens, even though these institutions are almost completely beyond the reach of democratic controls. Moreover, the European Council, which has energetically taken the initiative during the current crisis, is made up of heads of government whose role in the eyes of their citizens is to represent their respective national interests in distant Brussels. Finally, at least the European Parliament is supposed to establish a bridge between the political battles of opinions in the national arenas and the momentous decisions taken in Brussels. But there is hardly any traffic on this bridge.

Thus, to the present day there remains a gulf at the

European level between the citizens' opinion- and will-formation and the policies actually pursued for solving the pressing problems. This also explains why conceptions of the European Union and its future among the general population continue to be diffuse. Informed opinions and articulate positions on the direction of European development have to the present remained substantially the monopoly of professional politicians, economic elites and scholars with relevant interests; not even the intellectuals who usually participate in public debates have made this issue their own.[1] What currently unite European citizens are the Eurosceptical mindsets that have become more pronounced in all of the member countries during the crisis, albeit in each country for different reasons and for reasons that tend to polarize. Although this trend is an important factor to be taken into account by the political elites, the growing resistance is not really decisive for the actual course of European policymaking, which is largely uncoupled from the national arenas. The influential European political camps are forming in the circles that decide on the *policies* in accordance with controversial crisis diagnoses. The corresponding orientations reflect the well-known basic political orientations.

The European political groupings can be differentiated in accordance with preference variables that are located in two dimensions; it is a matter, on the one hand, of conflicting assessments of the importance of nation-states in an increasingly integrated and highly independent world society, and, on the other, of the familiar preferences for or against strengthening politics vis-à-vis the market. The fields of the cross-classification table that can be constructed by combining these pairs of attitudes towards the desired future of Europe yield, ideally speaking, four patterns of attitudes: among the defenders of national sovereignty, for whom even the decisions taken since May 2010 on the European

Stability Mechanism (ESM) and in the Fiscal Compact go too far, are, on the one hand, ordoliberal proponents of a lean nation-state and, on the other, republican or right-wing populist proponents of a strong nation-state. Among the proponents of the European Union and its progressive integration, by contrast, are, on the one side, economic liberals of various types and, on the other side, those who argue that the rampant financial markets should be tamed by supranational institutions. If we divide up the advocates of an interventionist policy once again according to where they are located on the left–right spectrum, we could distinguish among the Eurosceptics not only, as mentioned, between republicans or left communitarians and right-wing populists, but also within the integrationist camp between the Eurodemocrats and the technocrats. Of course, the Eurodemocrats should not be summarily equated with 'Eurofederalists', because their ideas on the desirable shape of a supranational democracy are not confined to the model of a European federal state.

The technocrats and the Eurodemocrats constitute, together with the Europe-friendly economic liberals, the temporary alliance of those who are pushing for deeper integration, though only the supranational democrats want to continue the unification process in order to bridge the gulf between *politics* and *policies* which is the decisive factor in the existing democratic deficit. All three factions have reasons for supporting the emergency measures adopted thus far to stabilize the single currency, whether out of conviction or willy-nilly. Most likely, however, this course is being pursued and implemented mainly by a further group of pragmatic politicians who follow an incrementalistic agenda. The politicians who wield power and decide on the course are moving without a comprehensive perspective towards 'More Europe', because they want to avoid the

far more dramatic and probably more costly alternative
of abandoning the euro.

From the perspective of our typology, however,
cracks are forming in this heterogeneous alliance. The
pragmatists who are setting the agenda in the short run
are allowing the snail's pace of reforms to be dictated
by short-term economic and everyday political 'imperatives', while the more far-sighted pro-European forces
are pulling in different directions. The market radicals
are primarily interested in relaxing the restrictions on
the European Central Bank's self-chosen refinancing
policy. The interventionists, buoyed by a tailwind from
the crisis-hit countries, are demanding that the austerity
course imposed by the German government be supplemented with targeted investment offensives. The
primary concern of the technocrats, meanwhile, is to
strengthen the decision-making power of the European
executive, while the Eurodemocrats defend different
models of a Political Union. Driven by different moti-
vations, these three forces are striving to supersede in
different directions the rickety status quo to which the
governments and political parties, which are under pressure to demonstrate their legitimacy, are clinging in the
face of growing Euroscepticism.

The dynamic of the conflicting motives shows that
the existing pro-European coalition will disintegrate as
soon as the unresolved problems compel the political
elites to view and deal with the crisis within an extended
time horizon. The road map for a deepening of the institutions of the Economic and Monetary Union drawn
up by the Commission, the President of the Council
and the Central Bank is testimony to the dissatisfaction
with the reactive nature of the existing approach. The
heads of government of the Eurozone initially requested
this plan, but immediately shelved it again, because
they shy away from grasping the hot iron of a formal
transfer of sovereignty rights to the European level. For

some, republican ties to the nation-state may still be too strong, whereas for others opportunistic motives of preserving their own positions of power may play a role. What pragmatists of all colours want to avoid, however, is another revision of the Treaty. For then how politics is conducted would have to be changed and European unification would have to be converted from an elite project into one that includes the citizens.[2]

(2) The Commission, the Presidency of the Council, and the European Central Bank (ECB) – known in Brussels parlance as 'the institutions' – are the least subject to legitimation pressures because of their relative distance from the national public spheres. So it was up to them to present proposals for the meeting of the European Council on 13 and 14 December 2012 that represent a brief and already diplomatically pared-down digest of a reform plan published a few days earlier by the Commission.[3] This is the first comprehensive document in which the EU develops a perspective for medium- and long-term reforms that goes beyond merely dilatory reactions to critical symptoms. Within this expanded time horizon, attention is no longer focused exclusively on the contingent constellation of causes that since 2010 has connected the global banking crisis with the vicious circle formed by the mutual refinancing of over-indebted European states and undercapitalized banks. Instead it directs attention to longer-term structural causes inherent in the monetary union itself.

The Economic and Monetary Union was designed in the 1990s in accordance with the ordoliberal ideas of the Stability and Growth Pact. It was conceived as a supporting pillar of an economic constitution which was supposed to stimulate free competition among market players across national borders and to be organized in accordance with general rules that were binding on all member states.[4] Even without the instrument of devaluing national currencies, which is not available in a monetary union, the differences in levels of competitiveness among the national economies were supposed to gradually even out. But the assumption that permitting unbridled competition subject to fair rules would lead to similar unit-labour costs and to equal levels of prosperity, thereby obviating the need for joint political decision-making on fiscal, budgetary and economic policy, has been proven wrong. Because the optimal conditions for a single currency in the Eurozone are not satisfied, the structural imbalances between the national economies that were there from the beginning have become more acute; and they will intensify further as long as the European policy pattern does not break with the principle of each member state making independent sovereign decisions on fiscal, budgetary and economic policy issues without taking other member states into consideration – in other words, from its national perspective alone.[5]

Despite some concessions, the German Federal Government has clung steadfastly to this dogma until now. The reforms adopted leave the sovereignty of the member states intact, if not de facto, then formally. The same holds for the stricter supervision of national budgetary policies, for the adoption of credit assistance instruments for heavily indebted states – the European Financial Stability Facility (EFSF) and the ESM – and for the planned establishment of a banking union and unified banking supervision under the auspices of the ECB (!). At most, the plans now under consideration for a uniform resolution of ailing banks, a transnational bank deposit protection fund and an EMU-wide transaction tax could be regarded as a first step towards a 'joint exercise of sovereignty by the individual states'.

Only the above-mentioned but provisionally shelved reform plan of the Commission addresses the actual cause of the crisis – namely, the faulty design of a monetary union that clings to the self-understanding of an alliance of sovereign states (or 'sovereign subjects of the Treaties'). According to this proposal, three essential, though vaguely defined, objectives are to be realized at the end of a tortuous reform path projected to last five years. *First*, there would be joint political decision-making at the EU level on 'integrated guidelines' for coordinating the fiscal, budgetary and economic policies of the individual states.[6] This would call for an agreement that prevents the policies of one member state from having negative external effects on the economy of another member state. *Second*, an EU budget based on the right to levy taxes, with a European financial administration, is envisaged for country-specific stimulus programmes. This would create scope for selective public investments through which the existing structural imbalances in the monetary union could be combated. *Third*, euro bonds and a debt repayment fund are supposed to make possible a partial collectivization of state debts. This would relieve the ECB of the task of preventing speculation against individual states in the Eurozone that it has currently assumed on an informal basis.

These objectives could be realized only if cross-border transfer payments with the corresponding transnational redistribution effects were accepted in the monetary union. From the perspective of the constitutionally required legitimation, therefore, the monetary union would have to be expanded into a real Political Union. The report of the Commission naturally proposes the European Parliament for this purpose and correctly states that closer 'interparliamentary cooperation as such does not . . . ensure democratic legitimacy for EU decisions'.[7] On the other hand, the Commission takes into account the reservations of the heads of state and adheres to the principle of radically exhausting the legal basis of the Lisbon Treaty so that the transfer of competences from the national to the European level can occur in a gradual and inconspicuous way. The aim is to postpone revising the Treaties to the very end of the reform period.[8] The new instruments that are designed to promote convergence in levels of competitiveness among the national economies[9] and to begin communalizing debts[10] are constructed in such a way that they preserve the fiction of continuing national budgetary autonomy.[11] However, the Commission pays a high price for the clever design of the smooth transitions from a supposed alliance of sovereign states to a Political Union.

(3) The problem is that the continuous series of reform steps obscures the required leap from the customary view of the political process, focused exclusively on one's own nation, to an inclusive perspective-taking that, from the viewpoint of each nation, accords equal consideration to citizens of the other nations. *Blurring this perspective* amounts to repudiating *the innovation* that has already begun in the institutions and procedures of the Union. When the so-called 'ordinary legislative procedure' is applied in the Union, it brings into alignment the results of political will-formation from two competing perspectives which are equally valid, though they are separately institutionalized. This procedure harmonizes the results of compromises between bargaining nation-states, on the one side, with those of a generalization of interests across national borders, on the other.

In the plans proposed by the Commission, this precise *expansion of the We-perspective of national citizens into one of European citizens*, which is constitutive for a proper European polity, is discreetly hidden away in a kind of appendix. To be sure, instilling this twofold perspective in the citizens, as a result of which political Europe would first appear in a different light, must be regarded as a process. But the enlargement of perspective has assumed an anticipatory institutional form with the elections to the European Parliament, and especially with the formation of Members of the European

Parliament into political groups. Nevertheless, the proposal of the Commission accords the expansion of steering capacities priority over a corresponding enlargement of the basis of legitimation also in the medium term. Thus *the delayed democratization* is presented as a promise in the manner of a light at the end of the tunnel. With this strategy the Commission is, of course, also serving the usual interest of the executive in expanding its power. But its primary objective seems to be to offer a platform on which groups with different political orientations can unite.

The incrementalism is a concession to the pragmatists, the expansion of supranational executive power a concession to the technocrats. An asymmetric Union with a strong, but free-floating, executive must be especially appealing to the market radicals. On paper, supranational democracy may be the declared long-term goal. However, if the economic constraints become intertwined with the flexibility of a free-floating European technocracy, it is probable that the unification process planned *for* but not *by* the people will grind to a halt before reaching the proclaimed goal. Without feedback from the insistent dynamics of a political public sphere and a mobilized civil society, political management lacks the drive to use the means of democratically enacted law to redirect the profit-oriented imperatives of investment capital into socially acceptable channels in accordance with the standards of political justice. This is why the functional benefits of an increase in the decision-making power of the European organs, without sufficient democratic oversight, would be problematic not only from the perspective of legitimation. The authorities would be predictably biased in favour of a particular pattern of politics.[12] A technocracy without democratic roots would have neither the power nor the motivation to accord sufficient weight to the demands of the electorate for social justice, status security, public services and collective goods, in the event of a conflict with the systemic demands for competitiveness and economic growth.

With the reform plan, all factions are served, just not the Eurodemocrats. To be sure, we find ourselves trapped in a dilemma between, on the one side, the economic policies required to preserve the euro and, on the other, the political steps towards closer integration. These necessary steps are unpopular and meet with spontaneous popular resistance. But the plans of the Commission reflect the temptation to bridge *in a technocratic manner* this gulf between what is economically required and what seems to be politically feasible. This approach harbours the danger of the gap between a consolidation of regulatory competences, on the one hand, and the need to legitimize these increased powers in a democratic manner, on the other, becoming still larger. Under the pull of this technocratic dynamic, the EU could align itself completely with the dubious ideal of a market-conforming democracy that would be even more meekly prey to the imperatives of the markets for want of an anchor in a politically mobilizable society. Then the national egoisms that the Commission would like to tame would form an explosive mixture with the technocratic governance exercised by 'people who enjoy the confidence of the markets'.[13]

In addition, the strategy of deferring democratization rests on an assumed sequence of short-, medium- and long-term reforms that is far from realistic. Admittedly, it is the chain of causes extending back to the foundation of the EMU that poses the real challenge. This calls for radical steps towards a genuine coordination of budgetary policies, with targeted programmes to boost national competitiveness, and the communalization of debts. But this is why the planning of these reforms must not be deferred to the long term out of deference to the fiction of still-intact national autonomy. What temporarily calmed the speculation in the financial markets, after all, was less the half-hearted rescue parachutes or the announcements of controls on national budgets than the 'financial firewall' that the head of the ECB, Mario Draghi, was able to establish with a single confidence-building announcement. Moreover, the Commission and Council can hardly finagle their way into a Political Union past the national public spheres without overstraining what is permissible under European law by centralizing existing competences in a series of incremental steps. Even the secondary legislation that authorizes the Commission to monitor budgets (through the Six Pack and Two Pack regulations) overdraws the legitimacy account of the existing Treaties and is rightly treated with suspicion by the national constitutional courts and parliaments.

(4) But what is the alternative to a further integration on the model of executive federalism? Let us first consider the political orientations that would have to stand at the beginning of the path leading to a democratically legitimized decision on the future of Europe. The three most important orientations are obvious:

(a) What is needed first of all is a consistent decision to expand the European Monetary Union into a Political Union that would remain open to the accession of other EU member states, in particular Poland. Although the Schengen Agreement and the introduction of the euro has already created a Union of different speeds, only this step would signify an internal differentiation of the Union into a core and a periphery. The implications for constitutional law would depend essentially on the behaviour of Great Britain, which is now even calling for certain European competences to be restored to the national level. What is to be feared and moreover cannot be excluded is a principled resistance which could be overcome only by a re-foundation of the Union (based on the existing institutions and developing them further).

(b) The decision in favour of a core Europe would amount to more than just a further evolutionary step in the transfer of individual sovereign rights. With the establishment of a joint fiscal, budgetary and economic policy, and especially with a harmonization of social policy, the red line of the classical understanding of sovereignty would be crossed. The idea that the nation-states are 'the sovereign subjects of the Treaties' would have to be abandoned. As the political role of the European Council during the present crisis and the decisions of the German Federal Constitutional Court show, this idea is more than a fiction. On the other hand, the step to supranational democracy need not be conceived as a transition to a 'United States of Europe'. 'Confederation' versus 'federal European state' is a false alternative (and a specific legacy of the constitutional discussion in nineteenth-century Germany).[14] The steering capacities which are missing at present, though they are functionally necessary for any monetary union, could and should instead be centralized within the framework of a *supranational*, yet *democratic*, political community. However, the nation-states should preserve their integrity as states within a supranational democracy by retaining their monopoly on the use of legitimate force and their function as the implementing administrations and as the final custodians of civil liberties.[15]

(c) At the procedural level, finally, the dethronement of the European Council, which still stands above the legislative process, means switching over from intergovernmentalism to the community method. As long as the ordinary legislative procedure, in which the Parliament and the Council participate on an equal footing, has not become the general rule, the EU shares a legitimacy deficit with all international organizations founded on treaties between states. This deficiency is explained by the asymmetry between the scope of the democratic mandate of the member states and the scale of the competences of the organization formed by all of them together.[16] Even the European Council would also inevitably become progressively more independent of its members without a switchover to a different mode of governance. For the closer the cooperation between the national executives becomes with the increasing scope and weight of its tasks, the less the decisions of the Council can be based exclusively on the kind of legitimation derived from the democratic character of its members. To the extent that the requirement of unanimity becomes hollowed out, even informally, supranational governance becomes synonymous with heteronomy. From the perspective of the national electorates, their political fate is then determined by foreign governments that represent the interests of other nations, rather than by a government that is bound by their democratic vote. This shortfall in legitimacy is exacerbated further by the fact that the negotiations are conducted out of the public eye.

The community method is preferable not only for this normative reason. It also contributes to effectiveness by helping to overcome national particularisms. In the Council, but also in inter-parliamentary committees, representatives who are obligated to defend national interests must negotiate compromises between the stubborn interests of the member states.[17] By contrast, the Members of the European Parliament, which is divided up into parliamentary groups, are elected on the basis of party preferences. This is why, to the extent that a European party system is taking shape, political decision-making can already be conducted in the European Parliament on the basis of interests generalized across national borders.

(5) These three fundamental orientations can be realized only through a change in primary law, which faces a high institutional hurdle. Therefore, the European Council – the institution that would have to overcome major difficulties for the procedural reasons mentioned in order to reach a consensus – would have to decide to convene a convention authorized to change the Treaty. On the one hand, the thought of their re-election is enough to make the heads of state recoil before this unpopular step; self-disempowerment is not in their interest either. On the other hand, they will not be able to ignore the economic constraints that will sooner or later force further integration, and hence a choice between the alternatives presented. For now, the German government is insisting that the individual state budgets be stabilized by the national administrations as a matter of priority and that this should be done at the expense of the national social security systems, public services and collective goods – in other words, at the expense of the already disadvantaged sections of the population. Together with a handful of smaller 'donor countries', Germany is vetoing the demand of the rest of the members for targeted investment programmes and for joint financial liability, which would lower the interest rates for the government bonds of the crisis-hit countries.

In this situation, the German government holds the keys to the fate of the European Union in its hand. If any one of the member states' governments is able to take the initiative to revise the Treaties, then the German government is. Of course, the other governments could call for solidarity-based assistance only if they were ready to take the constitutionally necessary complementary step of transferring sovereignty rights to the European level. Otherwise, any solidarity-based assistance would violate the democratic principle that the legislature that levies the taxes necessary for transfer payments must be identical with the institution that is responsible for the authorities in charge of allocating the funds. So the main question is not only whether Germany is in a position to take the corresponding initiative, but also whether it could have an interest in doing so.

Here my main concern is not the common interests of the member states – for example, the interest in the medium-term economic benefits of stabilizing the monetary union for all, or the interest in the self-assertion of a continent whose importance is diminishing compared to the growing economic weight of other world powers. The perception that global political power is shifting from West to East and the sense that the relationship with the United States is changing is casting a sharp light on the synergetic benefits of European unification. The role of Europe has changed in the postcolonial world not only when seen in the light of the dubious reputation of former imperial powers, not to mention the Holocaust. The statistical projections for the future also predict for Europe the fate of a continent with a shrinking population, decreasing economic weight and dwindling political importance. In view of these developments, European populations must recognize that the only way that they can maintain their social welfare model of society and the diversity of their national state cultures is through concerted action. They must join forces if they want to continue to exercise any influence at all over the agenda of international politics and the solutions to global problems. To renounce European unification would also be to turn one's back on world history.

These interests certainly form part of the equation

when it comes to Europe-wide will-formation concerning the goal of the unification process, which is not exhausted in economic benefits. But in the present context the issue is the interest of the state that, as things stand, should take the initiative: does Germany also have a special interest founded on its national history that goes beyond the common interest of the member states?

After the Second World War and the moral catastrophe of the Holocaust, the Federal Republic of Germany was on its knees and under a political and moral shadow. Thus prudential reasons of regaining the international reputation it had destroyed through its own actions alone made it imperative for Germany to promote a diplomatic alliance with France and to pursue European unification. Above all, however, the cautious cooperative policy of embedding itself in a context of neighbouring European countries solved a problem with deeper historical roots whose reappearance we have good reason to fear. After the foundation of the German Empire in 1871, Germany assumed a fateful 'semi-hegemonic status' in Europe – in the words of Ludwig Dehios, it was 'too weak to dominate the continent, but too strong to bring itself into line'.[18] It is clearly in Germany's interest to prevent a recurrence of this dilemma, which was overcome only thanks to European unification.

This is why the European question, which has been exacerbated by the crisis, also involves a domestic political challenge. The leadership role that now falls to Germany for demographic and economic reasons not only awakens historical memories all around us of the German occupation during the Second World War, but also fosters fatal notions within Germany itself. The consciousness of a recovered nation-state normality officially promoted since 1989–90 is double-edged. It is prone to becoming inflated into power fantasies that push in the direction either of a unilateral national course or of an equally questionable 'German Europe'. We Germans should have learned from the catastrophes of the first half of the twentieth century that it is in our national interest to permanently avoid the dilemma of a barely containable semi-hegemonic status. The real merit of Helmut Kohl is not the reunification, but the fact that this fortunate national occurrence was coupled with the consistent continuation of a policy that integrates Germany firmly into Europe.

In addition, there is the question of whether Germany not only has *interests* of its own in pursuing a policy of solidarity, but is also under an obligation to do so *for normative reasons*. Claus Offe appeals to three economic arguments in an attempt to demonstrate a normative obligation to perform acts of solidarity. To date, Germany has benefited the most from the single currency through increases in exports. Moreover, because of these export surpluses, Germany is contributing to exacerbating the economic imbalances within the monetary union and, as a contributory cause, is part of the problem. Finally, Germany is even profiting from the crisis itself, because the increase in interest rates for the government bonds of the over-indebted crisis-stricken countries is matched by a decrease in the interest rates on German government bonds.[19] In addition, the labour market is benefiting from the influx of young, well-trained people who do not see any future for themselves in the crisis-hit countries.

Admittedly, the normative premise that these asymmetric effects of the politically unregulated interdependencies between the national economies of the EU member states entail an obligation to act in solidarity is not that easy to explicate. And even if these arguments are cogent under the presupposition of retaining the European currency, opponents can avoid this obligation by citing the option of withdrawing from the euro, and that with a plausible normative argument of their own: because the establishment of the European Monetary Union was unanimously enacted at that time on the premise that it would not affect national budgetary autonomy, no party to the Treaty can now be required to take further steps towards a closer political union.

Given these arguments, in order to justify a plea for European solidarity one must eliminate ambiguities connected with the concept of solidarity itself. On the one hand, I would like to show that appeals to solidarity by no means rest on a confusion of politics with morality. This concept can and should be used in a genuinely political way. On the other hand, I would like to draw upon the history of the concept to remind us of the special context in which appeals to solidarity are appropriate. The decisive question then becomes how far the populations of the Eurozone now find themselves in a historic setting which calls for 'solidarity' in this sense.

(6) In view of the public sentiment in the civil societies of the euro countries, only the respective governments and the major political parties, aside from the labour unions which are likewise nationally fragmented, are for the present serious candidates for taking political initiatives. If they could bring themselves to take the risk of seriously confronting the electorate with European policy alternatives for the first time, they would be facing an unfamiliar task. Political parties are skilled in gimmicky ways of generating democratic legitimation that rely on opinion polls, and they are not ready to engage in processes of opinion- and will-formation that shape mentalities and deviate from established routines. This means that they are neither disposed to perceive extraordinary challenges in crisis situations nor ready to commit themselves to risky projects. These unfortunate circumstances do not make the infamous saying that 'individuals make history' any more true; but these cir-

cumstances lead one to ponder whether the right person at the right time could nevertheless influence historically momentous orientations in one way or another.

Be that as it may, the political parties would have to remember that democratic elections are not opinion polls, but the result of a process of forming a public will in which arguments carry weight. In a risky initial situation with sharply contrasting moods, majorities can be swung only by persistent discursive efforts, which in the present case continue over a legislative period. It is important in this context to clarify the status of the argument from solidarity. What count in social policy contexts are moral arguments of distributive justice, whereas in constitutional questions what count are juridical reasons. In order to exonerate appeals to solidarity from false accusations of being unpolitical, which so-called realists are wont to level against them, I would like to distinguish the obligation to show solidarity from obligations of a moral and legal kind.

Offering assistance out of solidarity is a political act that by no means calls for a form of moral selflessness that would be misplaced in political contexts. Konstantinos Simitis, Prime Minister of Greece at the time of its accession to the EU, wrote the following in the *Frankfurter Allgemeine Zeitung* on 27 December 2012:

> Solidarity is a concept that certain countries in the Union are not comfortable with. They associate it with an interpretation that concentrates exclusively on the need to support those countries that are not fulfilling their obligations. Yet reality necessitates a form of mutual support whose scope is not predefined by legal texts alone.[20]

The author argues that the European policy for which the German government is responsible fails to show solidarity. Even though Simitis is sitting in a glass house, his understanding of solidarity may nevertheless be correct. So: what is the meaning of solidarity?

Even though the two concepts are related, 'solidarity' is not synonymous with 'justice' either in the moral or the legal sense of the term. We call moral and legal norms 'just' when they regulate practices that are in the equal interest of all those affected. Just norms secure equal freedoms for all and equal respect for everyone. Of course, there are also special duties. Relatives, neighbours or colleagues can in certain situations expect more, or different kinds of, assistance from each other than from strangers. Such specific duties can also claim universal validity, even though they are restricted to certain social relations. Parents violate their duty of care, for example, when they neglect the health of their children. The extent of these positive duties is often indeterminate, of course; it varies according to the kind, frequency and importance of the corresponding social relations. When a distant relative contacts his surprised cousin again after decades with a request for a significant financial contribution because he is facing an emergency situation, he can hardly appeal to a moral – that is, a universally valid – obligation, but at best to a tie of an 'ethical' kind founded on family relations (in Hegel's terminology, one rooted in 'Sittlichkeit' or 'ethical life'). Membership of an extended family will ground an obligation only if the actual relation between those concerned generates the expectation that the cousin can in turn count on the support of her relative in a similar situation. In this case, it is the *trust-founding Sittlichkeit* of informal social relations that, subject to the condition of *predictable reciprocity*, requires that the one individual 'vouches' for the others.

Such 'ethical' obligations rooted in bonds of a preexisting community, typically in family ties, which must be distinguished from moral and legal obligations, exhibit three features. They ground exacting or 'supererogatory' claims that go beyond what an addressee would be obliged to do either by law or morality. On the other hand, when it comes to the required motivation for acting, this kind of ethical claim is less exacting than the categorical force of a moral duty; but it does not coincide with the kind of prudence or respect involved in obeying coercive law either. Moral commands should be obeyed out of respect for the underlying norm itself without regard to the future compliance of other persons, whereas the citizen's obedience to the law is conditional on the fact that the sanctioning power of the state ensures general compliance.[21] Fulfilling an ethical obligation, by contrast, can *neither be enforced nor categorically required*. It depends instead on the predictability of reciprocal conduct – and on confidence in this reciprocity over time.

In this respect, unenforceable ethical conduct also coincides with one's own medium- or long-term interest. It is precisely this aspect that 'Sittlichkeit' shares with 'solidarity', though the latter does not refer to pre-political communities, such as the family, but to political associations. What differentiates both ethical expectations and appeals to solidarity from law and morality is the peculiar reference to a 'joint involvement' in a network of social relations. That involvement grounds both another person's demanding expectations, which may even go beyond what law and morality command, and one's own confidence that the other will behave reciprocally in the future if need be.[22] Whereas 'morality' and 'law' refer to the equal freedoms of autonomous individuals, ethical expectations and appeals to solidarity refer to an interest in the integrity of a shared form of life that includes one's own well-being.[23] We should note, however, that, even though the concept of solidarity derives these semantic connotations from the memory of quasi-natural communities, such as families or corporations, it marks a change in the semantics of 'ethical life' proper in the following two respects.

Behaviour based on solidarity presupposes political contexts of life, hence contexts that are legally organized and in this sense artificial, not ones that have evolved 'organically'. Nationalism obscures this difference between 'solidarity' and pre-political 'Sittlichkeit'. It appeals without justification to the concept of solidarity when it champions 'national solidarity', and thereby assimilates the solidarity of the 'citizen' to cohesion among fellow-nationals.[24] This obscures the fact that the credit of trust that conduct based on solidarity can assume is less robust than in the case of ethical conduct. It cannot rely on the self-evidence of the conventional ethical relationships of a community that evolved in a quasi-natural way. What lends behaviour based on solidarity a distinctive character more than anything else is, secondly, the *offensive character* of striving or even struggling to discharge the promise invested in the legitimacy claim of any political order. This character comes to the fore especially in the wake of economic modernization processes when acting in solidarity is needed to widen the overstrained forms of integration of a political order that has been overrun – that is, in order to adapt to more comprehensive, systemic interdependencies, which make themselves felt to the citizens only indirectly, as restrictions on their political self-determination. In what follows, I will explain the two dimensions of the meaning of the concept – first, the reference to political contexts of life and, second, the abstract character of confidence in a form of reciprocity vouched for by legally organized relations.

(7) The customary talk of 'civic solidarity' presupposes the legally constituted social environment of a political community, normally a nation-state. The outrage over violations of civic solidarity finds expression, for example, in anger over tax evaders who weasel their way out of their responsibility for the political community while unashamedly enjoying its advantages.

Tax evasion is admittedly also a breach of established law. However, the resentment against these free riders is an expression of the same disappointed expectation of solidarity as is expressed in the contempt for all of the tax-evading Depardieus of this world who *legally* transfer their place of residence or the headquarters of their company abroad. As can be seen from the development of the welfare state, expectations of solidarity can become transformed into legal claims.[25] Even today, how much inequality the citizens of a wealthy country want to live with is still a question of solidarity and not of law. It is not the constitutional state that curbs the growing numbers of young people out of work, of the long-term unemployed and of people in precarious employment, of elderly people whose pension is barely enough for survival, or of impoverished single mothers who have to rely on what are in effect soup kitchens. Only the policy of a legislator who is responsive to the normative claims of a democratic civic community can transform the claims to solidarity of the marginalized or their advocates into social rights.[26]

Notwithstanding the differences between solidarity, on the one hand, and law and morality, on the other, there is a close conceptual connection between 'political justice' and solidarity.[27] In Portugal at the turn of 2012/13, the conservative president Aníbal Cavaco Silva called upon the constitutional court to scrutinize the government's austerity budget passed by the members of his own party, because he considered the social consequences of the policy model imposed by the creditors (in particular, the one-sided impositions on civil servants, public-service employees, social security recipients and pensioners, quite apart from the shattered career expectations of the younger generations) to be untenable from the perspective of political justice. In doing so, the president translated into the language of political justice the street protests that in all of the crisis-hit countries are demanding solidarity from the indigenous elites and the so-called donor countries. The more unjust the *political* circumstances, the more the disadvantaged have reason to demand solidarity on the part of the privileged. However, calls for solidarity refer to a form of social cohesion that is not easy to define. The degree of social integration that is politically required is not exhausted by quantifiable factors; social anomie represents the limit case of social disintegration. Therefore, questions of political justice and solidarity are always matters of more or less, whereas the binary questions of moral and legal justice call for a 'Yes' or a 'No'.

These conceptual relations show that 'solidarity' (in contrast to 'ethical life') does not refer to an existing social context but to one which, although presupposed, has to be *created through politics*. This offensive semantic component, in addition to the reference to politics, only becomes clear when we make the transition from unhistorical conceptual clarification to the history of ideas. Surprisingly, the concept of solidarity is an astonishingly recent one, whereas disputes over 'right' and 'wrong' were conducted in the archaic civilizations, hence since the third millennium BCE. Although the word 'solidarity' can be traced back to the Roman law of debts, only since the French Revolution of 1789 did it acquire a political meaning, albeit at first in connection with the slogan of 'fraternity'. The battle cry of *fraternité* is a product of the humanist generalization of a consciousness engendered by the major world religions; it goes back to the perspective-widening experience that one's own local community is part of the universal community of all believers. This is the background of fraternity as the key concept of a secular religion of humanity that was radicalized and fused with the concept of solidarity during the first half of the nineteenth century by early socialism and Catholic social teaching, and slightly later by social democracy, with reference to the current social question. Even Heine had still used the concepts 'fraternity' and 'solidarity' more or less synonymously in the pre-March period.[28] The two concepts became separated in the course of the social upheavals of approaching industrial capitalism and the nascent workers' movement. The legacy of the Judeo-Christian ethics of fraternity forged an alliance in the concept of solidarity with the republicanism of Roman origin. The Judeo-Christian orientation towards salvation or emancipation became amalgamated with the Roman orientation towards legal and political freedom.[29]

The concept arose in a situation in which revolutionaries were suing for solidarity in the sense of a *redemptive reconstruction* of relations of solidarity that were familiar but had become hollowed out by the more far-reaching processes of modernization.[30] The early socialism of deracinated journeymen drew its utopian energies also in part from unrealistic nostalgic memories of the paternalistically secluded lifeworld of the guilds. At that time, an accelerated functional differentiation of society gave rise to extensive interdependencies behind the backs of a paternalistic, still largely corporative and occupationally stratified everyday world. Under the pressure of these reciprocal functional dependencies the older forms of social integration broke down and led to the rise of class antagonisms, which were finally contained within the extended forms of political integration of the nation-state. The appeals to 'solidarity' had their historical origin in the dynamic of the new class struggles. The well-founded appeals to solidarity of the new forms of organization of the workers' movement were a reaction to the fact that the systemic constraints had outstripped the old relations of solidarity. The socially uprooted journeymen, workers, employees and day labourers were supposed to form an alliance beyond the systemically produced competitive relations on the labour market.

The opposition between social classes of industrial capitalism acquired an enduring institutional form only within the framework of the democratically constituted nation-states. In the course of economic globalization, these European states, which assumed their present-day form of welfare states only after the catastrophes of the two world wars, find themselves exposed once again to the explosive pressure of economic interdependencies that tacitly permeate national borders. It is in turn systemic constraints that shatter the established relations of solidarity and compel us to reconstruct the intricate forms of political integration of the nation-state. This time, the politically unregulated systemic contingencies of a form of capitalism driven by unleashed financial markets are becoming condensed into tensions between the member states of the European Monetary Union. The expectation of solidarity voiced by Konstantinos Simitis acquires its legitimacy from this historical perspective.

He explicitly refers to the network of long-established interdependencies that must now be brought under control in reconstructed forms of political integration from the normative perspective of a fair balancing of the contingent advantages and disadvantages among the member states. If we want to preserve the monetary union, it is no longer enough, given the structural differences between the national economies, to provide loans to over-indebted states so that each can increase its competitiveness through its own efforts. What is required is instead a cooperative effort from a shared political perspective to promote growth and competitiveness in the Eurozone as a whole. Such an effort would require Germany to accept short- and medium-term negative redistributive effects in its longer-term self-interest. That would be an exemplary case of political solidarity in the sense outlined.

2

European Citizens and European Peoples

The Problem of Transnationalizing Democracy

I use the term 'transnationalization' to refer to the process that aims to create a 'supranational' democracy, that is, one above the organizational level of a state. Taking the European Union as a model, 'supranational' is meant to express the idea that such a polity assumes a federal character, but – unlike federal states – not the familiar characteristics of a state. This supranational construct is not supposed to enjoy either a monopoly over the legitimate use of force or ultimate decision-making authority. Instead it should be based on the weak priority of the application of federal law and leave the implementation of statutes, guidelines and decrees to the governments of the member states. Can such a union satisfy the standards of democratic legitimacy that we are familiar with from nation-states? I think that this question is important not only when it comes to the future of the European Union, but also when one considers the current threat to the democratic substance of all nation-states, especially the smaller ones.

Our era is marked by a growing mismatch between a world society that is becoming increasingly interdependent at the systemic level and a world of states that remains fragmented. The states, which are consciously integrated by their citizens, remain the only collectives capable of taking effective action based on democratic decisions and of intentionally protecting and shaping the social conditions of their populations. But they are becoming more and more deeply entangled in systemic relationships that permeate national borders. Above all, globalized markets make use of accelerated digital communication to create ever denser networks and bring these collective actors into completely new kinds of dependencies. In view of the politically undesirable side effects of systemic integration, there is a need for steering that single nation-states are increasingly unable to meet. Politicians and citizens sense this loss of political decision-making power and, in a psychologically understandable but paradoxical defensive reaction, cling even more firmly to the nation-state and its borders, even though these have long since become porous.

The national scope for action that has already been lost and is still shrinking can be made good only at the supranational level. Indeed, this is actually happening in the form of international cooperation. The rapidly increasing number of influential international organizations has given rise to a variety of forms of governance beyond the nation-state. But these international treaty regimes largely escape proper democratic control.[1] An alternative would be to form supranational communities that, as I will show, can in principle satisfy democratic standards of legitimacy even when they do not assume the format of states writ large. One need not share Marxist background assumptions to recognize in the unleashing of financial markets and the 'financialization' of capitalism one of the crucial reasons for this development[2] – and to conclude that we must first implement a promising re-regulation of the global banking sector within an economic region of at least the size and importance of the Eurozone.[3] In Europe, these problems have come to a particularly drastic head as a result of the high level of economic integration that we have achieved.

I will first discuss the crisis management, which, although it has left the core of the problems untouched, has led to a self-empowerment of the European executive. The resulting shortfalls in legitimation, no less than the unsolved problem of structural economic imbalances, call for deeper integration in the Eurozone at least (1). Against the background of these current developments, I will then turn to the theoretical question of how a supranational polity can satisfy the principle of democracy that has hitherto been realized only in the nation-state format (2). Taking the example of how the United States arose, I will discuss the constitutional problem that must be solved in the process of European integration if the EU, or at least a Euro-Union, is one day to measure up to its own aspirations (3). On the other hand, the most important resource – namely, mutual trust between the European peoples – is lacking, even if one disregards the national prejudices that were first stirred up during the crisis. At the same time, we must also recognize that the fear of a superstate mainly betrays the desire to hold on to the democratic substance guaranteed by one's own nation-state. A democratically organized Union could take this justified insistence on a normative achievement into account (4). Therefore, I will suggest a counterfactual scenario of constitution-making, according to which the European peoples would participate together with the totality of the European citizens on an equal footing. This hypothetically assumed perspective reveals the innovative ways in which the European Union is already moving in the direction of a transnational democracy, as well as the reforms that would still have to be made in order to turn the existing Union into a democracy (5). In conclusion, I will briefly examine some implications for the theory of democracy of the unfamiliar proposal of two subjects engaging simultaneously in constituting a trans-national democracy (6).

(1) First, some observations on a still unsolved problem that for the moment prevents a lasting stabilization of the Eurozone. It was possible to avert the sovereign debt crisis only because the ECB managed to present a credible simulation of joint liability – that is, a fiscal sovereignty that the Union in fact lacks because of the ban on a bailout. Nevertheless, the ECB's lack of repayment responsibility is not the essential design flaw of the monetary union. Economists have long been warning about the sub-optimal conditions that the Eurozone offers for a common currency area.[4] Because of the real economic differences between the current account balances of the different national economies, uniform interest rates send the national governments the wrong signals. *One size for all fits no one.* The structural differences among the economies of the member states mean that their performance will drift further apart unless a joint economic government is established.

It is a well-known fact that the European Council has pursued an investor-friendly policy that, aside from necessary administrative and labour-market reforms, confines itself to dictating austerity measures to the crisis-plagued countries – requirements that weigh exclusively on wages, social benefits, the civil service and public infrastructure. The Council imposes conditions on national governments that amount to treating the citizens of democratic polities like minors. Instead, the design flaw of a monetary union without a political union should have been tackled. Without the institutional framework for jointly coordinated fiscal and economic policies (with implications for a common social policy), the structural imbalances between the different economies are destined to increase. Therefore, the economic constraints speak in favour of a reform that would put the Council and the European Parliament in a position to make joint decisions on federal guidelines for fiscal, economic and social politics. But the governments of the donor countries, in particular the German government, lack the courage to canvass support for solidaristic measures among their electorates.

The pattern of offloading problems on to pseudo-sovereign member states has an ironic reverse side – the power of the executive bodies has actually grown. The crisis management under German leadership has necessitated a self-empowerment of the governments assembled in the Euro Group. In an alliance with the European executive branch (comprising the Council, the Commission and the ECB), they have extended their scope for action at the cost of the national parliaments, and in the process have greatly exacerbated the existing shortfalls in legitimacy.[5] The European Parliament did not have any share in the increase in competences generated by the momentous reform measures of recent years – the Fiscal Compact, the European Stability Mechanism (ESM) and the so-called Six Pack – even when it participated in the legislative process. To this day, there is a lack of a counterpart in the European Parliament that mirrors the powerful Euro Group in the Council. Without a standing committee for the members from the Eurozone, the Parliament cannot even properly exercise its monitoring rights, which are in any case far too weak.

In this complicated situation, the theoretical question of the possibility of a transnationalization of democracy in the shape of a polity that is both federal and supranational acquires immediate political relevance. In the academic literature one finds repeated attempts to solve this persistent problem by recourse to semantic cosmetics. There is no lack of proposals that cast the existing democratic deficits in a flattering light through a shrewd reduction of democratic standards.[6] Therefore, I would first like to explain briefly the concept of democracy properly understood.

(2) With the self-empowerment of the National Assembly, the French Revolution facilitated an exemplary breakthrough of the principle of democracy in the shape of a unitary state. Within this national framework, the revolutionary constitutions were able to realize the principle of the self-legislation of a nation of free and equal citizens differently than in federations. Democratic self-determination means that the addressees of coercive laws are subject only to the laws that they have enacted for themselves through a democratic process. This procedure owes its legitimizing force, on the one hand, to the inclusion of all citizens in political decision-making (however this is mediated) and, on the other, to the linking of political decisions with a deliberative mode of public opinion formation and parliamentary deliberation.[7]

Legitimate state power proceeds from the 'people', but only in the constitution-building process do the people exercise their authority in an *undivided* way. This idea is expressed in the concept of popular sovereignty.[8] At the level of the *constituted* political authority, by contrast, the citizens exercise their sovereignty only through the channels of a *division of powers*; legislative power is supplemented by judicial and administrative powers. Within the constitutional state, popular sovereignty is dispersed and emerges from its latency only when it comes to changing the constitution.

The same principle of democracy was realized in a different way in the shape assumed by the United States since 1789, namely, within a federation of states. Here a democratic federation emerged from a confederation of individual states that had seceded from the British Empire. Over the course of the nineteenth century, this federation – not unlike Switzerland after its constitutional revolution in 1848 – developed into a national federal state with features clearly distinct from the earlier forms of a *confederation of states*.

The problem that arises in every federal entity is the interpenetration of the *international relations between* the member states with the national organization of political will-formation *within* each of the states. International law and the concept of a contract, on the one side, and state law and the concept of a national constitution, on the other side, intermingle in all federations. But in the early modern confederations, the integration of the legal relations between the states and the national legal systems of the member states remained superficial. In the controversies recorded in the 'Federalist Papers', by contrast, one can trace the chief issue at stake in the development from a confederation into a democratic federal state – namely, how the democratic character of an alliance of member states *each of which has already been democratically constructed* can be preserved.[9]

(3) An alliance of *democratic* states not only affects the relation between national *governments* and the federal institutions, as was the case in the early federations; rather, the *peoples themselves* have to pool their 'sovereignties'. With the founding of the United States, the integration of states had crossed the historical threshold of an integration not just of governments but also of the participating 'peoples'. For this reason, the international legal principle of the equality of states here for the first time served a different function, namely, to ensure the equal status of the peoples of democratic member states in a second chamber, the Senate. The principle of 'state equality', hitherto a principle of international law, was if you like domesticated for the purpose of securing the equal representation of member states in a democratic federal state. In international law, it guarantees an equal standing of states and governments; but within a federal state it protects, together with an equal standing of

member states, simultaneously the democratic rights of the peoples of each of the states.

Insofar as the colonial states, which had just fought for their independence, regarded themselves as the subjects of the constitution-building process, it was only logical not to communalize the constitution-amending powers of the individual states completely, but to reserve decisive veto positions for the states in the federation. On the other hand, insofar as the entire future citizenry of the union recruited from the individual states regarded *itself* as the true constitution-framing subject, there was no obstacle to the constitution of a federal state. From a legal point of view, this alternative was ultimately decided in favour of the federation. As is well known, agreement was reached on Article V of the US Constitution, which, instead of *unanimity*, only requires the approval of a *majority* of the legislatures of the individual states to change the Constitution. This provision can be understood, retrospectively at any rate, as a pointer in the direction of a federal state.[10]

We can learn two things from this development for the comparison with a supranational democracy composed of nation-states such as the EU. Bringing the two competing principles of the equality of states and the equality of citizens into harmony within the framework of a nation-state was the invention of a two-chamber system and a corresponding division of powers. The Senate or second chamber can ensure a suitable form of participation in federal legislation through the competing legislation of the member states. The principle of democracy finds full application in such a federal state precisely in virtue of the fact that the principle of state equality is adequately embodied in the second chamber. For only in this way are the citizens of the member states, which are themselves democratically structured, invested with the right to a form of democratic participation that is indirect but of equal weight. However, it is not the case that each individual state can claim the last word on changing the Constitution. Thus, the first thing that is needed for a proper federal state is the normative subordination of the states to the federal level. Second, that priority of the federal level over the individual states expresses the political identity of the people from which all political authority proceeds: it is in the final analysis the national citizenry as a whole that establishes and sustains a democratic federal state – not the governments of the several states or their citizens.

(4) As it happens, the citizens in Europe don't want to fulfil either of these conditions. They don't want a large-scale federal state. The peoples who took part in the establishment of the United States were composed of immigrants who had liberated themselves from the colonial rule of their common mother country; by contrast, the peoples who are playing a decisive role in the European project have been living in 'old' nation-states for centuries. There are many reasons why the process of European unification is stalled. But the main one is the lack of the mutual trust that the citizens of different nations would have to show each other as a precondition for their willingness to adopt a common perspective that transcends national boundaries when making political decisions on federal issues. And yet this lack of trust should not be located in the wrong place. Nationalism confuses two forms of solidarity that we must distinguish today. We should not confuse the informal solidarity that habitually develops in families and pre-political communities with *legally constituted civic* solidarity.

In European states that emerged from national unification movements, a national consciousness was fostered, indeed produced, by schools, the military, national historiography and the press. It became superimposed on older dynastic and religious ties, as well as regional forms of life and loyalties. As we can see in many places today, conflicts continually flare up around these older regional and ethnic boundaries in times of crisis, conflicts that awaken older loyalties and can lead to the disintegration of national solidarity. But we should not be enticed into drawing hasty parallels between these sorts of conflicts and the role that the nation-states are currently playing in blocking the European integration process.

Nations are composed of citizens and form political communities that did not develop spontaneously, but were instead legally constructed. Contrary to the ethno-national ideologies that try to suppress this fact, the political level of civic integration here acquires a weight entirely of its own compared to the informal layers of sociocultural integration.[11] Unlike the loyalty to a territorial lord, which rests on existing forms of *social integration*, national consciousness, including the ascriptive characteristics attributed to it *retrospectively*, is the result of an organized form of *political integration*.

Viewed historically, a relatively high level of political inclusion has been achieved in the meantime; and we have to keep this political level in mind if we want to explain the lack of mutual trust between the national populations. The lack of trust that we presently observe between European nations is not primarily an expression of xenophobic self-isolation against foreign nations, but instead reflects in the first place the insistence of self-conscious citizens on the *normative* achievements of their respective nation-states. In present-day Europe, there is a widespread conviction that national citizens owe the fragile resource of free and relatively equitable living conditions to the democratic practices and liberal institutions of their states. Therefore, they have a well-founded interest in 'their' nation-states remaining guarantors of these achievements and not being exposed to the risk of intrusions and encroachments by an unfamiliar supranational polity. Their suspicion is directed more against the supranational paternalism of a superstate than against the forms of life and mentalities of neighbouring peoples rejected as foreign.

This is why the lack of a 'European people' is not the insurmountable obstacle to joint political decision-making it is sometimes alleged to be. Indeed, translingual citizenship uniting such a numerous variety of different language communities *is* a novelty. But Europeans already share the principles and values of largely overlapping political cultures. What is required is a European-wide political communication. For this we need a European public sphere, which does not mean a new one, however. The existing national public spheres suffice for this purpose; they only have to open themselves up sufficiently *to each other*. And the existing national media are sufficient, too, provided they perform a complex task of translation: they must learn also to report on the discussions being conducted in the other countries on the issues of common concern to all citizens of the Union.[12] Then the trust among citizens that currently exists in the form of a nationally limited civic solidarity can very well develop into an even more abstract form of trust that reaches across national borders.[13]

The 'no demos' thesis obscures a factor that we must take seriously – the conviction that the *normative* achievements of the democratic state are worth preserving. This self-assertion of a democratic civil society is something different from the reactive clinging to naturalized characteristics of ethno-national origin that provides sustenance to right-wing populism. In addition, democratic self-assertion is not only an empirical motive, but also a justifying reason that, under the present circumstances, speaks *for* the attempt to realize a supranational democracy. It is not as if democracies shut up in nation-states could preserve their democratic substance, as though they were unaffected by involvement in the systemic dynamics of a global society – at any rate not, as indicated, in Europe.

Let me summarize. European citizens have good reasons to pursue two competing goals simultaneously: on the one hand, they want the Union that has arisen from nation-states to assume the form of a supranational polity that can act effectively in a democratically legitimate way; on the other hand, they want to embark on this transnationalization of democracy only under the proviso that their nation-states, in their role as future member states, remain *guarantors of the already achieved level of justice and freedom*. In the supranational polity, the higher political level should not be able to overwhelm the lower one. The issue of ultimate decision-making authority should not be resolved through hierarchization, as it is in federal states. The supranational federation should instead be constructed in such a way that the heterarchical relationship between the member states and the federation remains intact.

(5) To solve this problem, I propose a thought experiment. Let us imagine a democratically developed European Union *as if* its constitution had been brought into existence by a double sovereign.[14] The constituting authority should be composed of the entire citizenry of Europe, on the one hand, and of the peoples of Europe, on the other. Already during the constitution-framing process, the one side should be able to address the other side with the aim of achieving a balance between the corresponding interests. In that case, the heterarchical relationship between European citizens and European peoples would structure the founding process itself. The competition over interests between the two constitution-founding subjects would then be reflected at the level of the *constituted* polity in procedures that require agreements between two legislative bodies with equal rights – such as the European Parliament and the Council.

In this scenario the doubled sovereign can no longer decide in a really sovereign manner. For the 'levelling up' of the European citizens through the addition of the

European peoples indicates that the sovereign must have already committed itself from the outset to recognizing the historical achievements of a level of justice embodied by the nation-states. 'Higher-level' or 'shared' sovereignty means that the constituting authority is limited by an obligation to conserve from a revolutionary past within the larger frame of the future Union the substance of what national citizens claim as the emancipatory achievements of their respective national democracies.

If one asks from this perspective of a 'double' sovereign which further reforms of the existing European Treaties are necessary to eliminate the existing legitimation deficits of the European Union in its present state – then the answer is obvious. The European Parliament would also have to be able to introduce legislative initiatives, and the so-called 'ordinary legislative procedure', which requires the approval of both chambers, would have to be extended to all policy fields. In addition, the European Council – thus the assembly of heads of government who to this day enjoy a semi-constitutional status – would have to be incorporated into the Council of Ministers. Finally, the Commission would have to assume the functions of a government answerable to Council and Parliament in equal measure. With this transformation of the Union into a supranational polity that satisfies democratic standards, the principles of the equality of states and of the equality of citizens would be accorded equal consideration. The democratic will of the two constitution-framing subjects would be reflected in the symmetrical participation of both 'chambers' in the legislative process and in the symmetrical status of Parliament and Council with respect to the executive branch.

Such a radically reformed Union would still deviate considerably from the model of a federal state. Interestingly enough, current EU law includes a range of important provisions that, on the assumption of a sovereignty shared by European citizens and peoples, can be understood as legitimate deviations from the federal state model:

- the requirement of consensus among member states for any ordinary change of the Treaties;
- the right of member states to leave the Union, where the qualifications governing the process of exit throw an interesting light on how the original sovereignty of the acceding state had been 'divided', but not completely 'forfeited';
- the right of review to which the national constitutional courts lay claim in order to prevent European law falling below the level achieved in the member states;
- the principle of limited conferral of powers, which ensures that European institutions do not acquire ultimate decision-making authority;
- strong competences of the member states in implementing European decisions, which prevent the supranational polity from acquiring the character of a state;
- primacy of European law over the national legal systems which is justified only in functional terms and not by the general priority of federal over national competencies; and
- the decentralized monopoly over the use of legitimate force, which remains with the member states.

These principles and provisions can be understood from a reconstructive perspective as a logical expression of democratic will-formation in a constituent assembly that has a heterogeneous composition in the sense outlined. To this extent, the European Treaties already prefigure an at once federally and democratically constituted supranational polity.

(6) With this step, the democratic legitimation of the constituted polity is shifted from the level of the

constitution-building process to *the meta-level of the justification for the peculiar composition of the constituent authority* itself. The citizens of a future European Union taken as a whole are willing to share equal rights with the peoples of the future member states, while the 'peoples' are willing to participate in the project in turn only on the condition that, in the supranational political community to be established, the integrity of their states in their role as guarantors of the historically achieved levels of freedom and justice is assured. Even though the totalities of 'citizens' and 'peoples' overlap exactly, so that they are composed of the same persons, the willingness on both sides to accept these terms does not fall from the sky – neither the concession made by the future European citizens to restrict their sovereignty in favour of the involvement of European peoples, nor the reservation that the latter make by insisting on the normative substance of their respective national states. Seeping down from the abstract level of political theory to the turbulent waves of history, such an agreement, which Europeans must reach among themselves, can be brought about only by a painful learning process.

From the perspective of democratic theory, which I chose to adopt in this essay, the agreement by the two sides to cooperate in founding a constitution opens up a new dimension. Such a process, one which precedes the actual process of constitution-making, is reminiscent of the controversy recorded in the Federalist Papers. However, this discussion had a different outcome: the result of a long process was the first democratically legitimized federal state.

We are currently engaged in a discussion in the European Union that is similar in some respects. To judge by the course of our present discussion, however, it does not seem possible to resolve the tension-laden relationship between the two subjects – the citizens of the separate states and the future citizens of the Union

– in favour of a hierarchical arrangement. The best that we can hope for is to throw light on two competing objectives that the respective proponents regard as non-negotiable.

The formation of a federation composed of nation-states is already de facto far advanced; under the pressure of the problems of the banking and sovereign debt crisis, it is now a matter of how this project can be brought to a conclusion in such a way that the conflicting goals can be achieved simultaneously: the supranational polity that is empowered to act in important policy fields should, on the one hand, be allowed to exercise its jurisdiction only in democratically legitimate ways, without, on the other hand, depriving the member states of the measure of autonomy that allows them to ensure *themselves* that the normative substance that our national democracies embody is conserved.

The best outcome that can be hoped for is that the citizens satisfy their two allegiances when they press ahead with the integration process from the perspective *as if they had* participated in the constitution-building process from the outset *as equal subjects* in their dual role as future citizens of the Union and as current national citizens. If this shared intention of both parties could be reconstructed in addition as if it were the result of a process of democratic opinion- and will-formation, then the last remaining gap in the chain of legitimation would be closed in our scenario.

For from the viewpoint of political theory, this 'higher-level' constitutional process is different from all that have gone before. Following in the footsteps of the two constitutional revolutions of the late eighteenth century, many more constitutional states have been founded right up to the present day. All of these constitutional foundations can be understood (at the requisite level of abstraction) as a replication of the two original constitutive acts in Philadelphia and Paris. As we can now see, the creation of a supranational democracy, by contrast, cannot be understood on the model of a *two-stage* process according to which the constitutional democracies are a product of the constitution-framing process. More suitable here is instead a *three-stage model* in which the existence of democratically constituted nation-states is already presupposed. With the citizens who want to defend the historical achievement of constitutional revolutions, a subject comes into play that now empowers itself to serve as another constituting authority.

With the prior constitution of a higher-level sovereignty itself – hence, with the agreement between the two designated constitution-building subjects – the classical picture of a constituting and a constituted level is supplemented by a further dimension that once again underlies the actual constitution-building process.

3

Keywords on a Discourse Theory of Law and of the Democratic Constitutional State[1]

I have been asked first to review some of my motives for choosing the discourse-theoretical approach that I developed in *Between Facts and Norms* (1–4), and then to address some perspectives from which this approach might also provide pointers for conceptualizing the constitutionalization of international law (5–10).

(1) The more the complexity of society and of the problems in need of political regulation increases, the less it seems to be possible to cling to the demanding idea of democracy according to which the addressees of the law should at the same time be its authors. Even at a first glance, the incrementalistic mode of politics of an executive that merely reacts to the imperatives of stubborn functional systems, and as a result uncouples its choice of policies as much as possible from the legitimation process, seems to speak against this idea. But even under these conditions, a communication-theoretical approach can continue to lend a certain plausibility to the democratic promise of inclusion, that is, to the

46

participation of all citizens in the political process. We must not restrict elections and plebiscites to the act of voting. Votes acquire the institutional weight of decisions of co-legislators only in conjunction with a vital public sphere, that is, with the dynamics of the pros and cons of free-floating opinions, arguments and positions.

Political elections are different from opinion polls; they should not only reflect a spectrum of existing preferences. Because the digital revolution represents just a further step in the communicative networking and mobilization of civil society, we must abandon an institutionally frozen picture of the constitutional state. The communicative dissolution of politics can provide the key to a sociological analysis of what is realistic in the concept of *deliberative politics*.[2] And from this point of view the construction of the constitutional state can also be understood as a network of legally institutionalized discourses in which opinions and a collective will take shape.

(2) A further, more philosophical, reason for choosing the discourse-theoretical approach is the resolution of the paradox generated by the type of legitimacy that Max Weber calls 'legal rule': how is the emergence of legitimacy from mere legality supposed to be possible? What lends a completely positivized legal system legitimacy if everything counts as law that has been produced in accordance with a positively codified procedure? The answer of legal positivism is to fall back on an arbitrarily adopted or customary basic rule as a premise that grounds validity. Natural law, by contrast, appeals to privileged access to knowledge of unconditionally valid – because cosmologically anchored or theologically grounded – laws. The voluntarist explanation misses the cognitive content of belief in legitimacy; the natural law-based explanation rests on metaphysical worldviews that are not persuasive for everyone in pluralistic societies.

In contrast to both of these approaches, discourse theory attributes legitimizing force to the process of democratic opinion- and will-formation *itself*. This legally institutionalized procedure grounds a fallible presumption that decisions are rational when it roughly meets two conditions: the equal inclusion of all those affected, or their representatives, and the connection of the democratic decision back to an informal discursive exchange of relevant topics and contributions (that is, of information, reasons and opinions). According to this conception, the normative source of legitimacy springs from the combination of the inclusion of all those affected and the deliberative character of their opinion- and will-formation. Therefore, the idea of the free formation of a shared will guided by reason (that is, of a result that is accepted as one that has been achieved in common, following a consensual procedure of deliberation and decision-making) finds expression in the combination of inclusion and deliberation.

(3) A third motive for choosing the discourse-theoretical approach is to bridge the prima facie antagonism between two principles of legitimacy, 'popular sovereignty' and the 'rule of law'. In the history of political theory, the proponents of liberalism and republicanism argue over what should have priority: the liberty of the moderns – that is, the subjective freedoms of citizens in modern market-based societies; or the liberty of the ancients – that is, the political participation rights of democratic citizens. Each of these alternatives has unfortunate consequences: either the laws (including the constitution) are legitimate only if they are consistent with human rights stipulated in advance by morality, in which case the democratic legislator cannot make legitimate decisions in a sovereign way, but only within imposed constraints; or laws (including the constitution) are always legitimate when they are the product of democratic will-formation. In that case, however, the sovereign people could give itself any arbitrary constitu-

tion and enact any arbitrary norms, so that breaches of the norms of the rule of law cannot be ruled out.

In contrast, the discourse-theoretical justification of a system of rights can point a way out of the impasse and do justice to the intuition that democracy and the rule of law are co-original. Assuming that the constitution-founding subjects intend to establish a voluntary association of free and equal legal consociates in a deliberative manner *in the language of modern law*, then they can make their first sovereign decision only after they have clarified *in the abstract* what types of subjective freedoms of action they must confer on each other before they can legitimately regulate any given matter *by means of modern law*. Without the intention to confer on each other rights of the kind found in the familiar classical categories of basic rights, the constitutional legislator would even lack the medium – that is, the language – required in order to make legitimate law. (4) A final motive is to settle an unsatisfying dispute between the liberal and social welfare paradigms of law. The basic conceptual structure of this dispute is reminiscent of the division of roles through which the deontological understanding of modern law differs from the deontological understanding of morality. According to the Kantian idea of autonomy, people act freely when they *obey* just those laws that they have *given themselves* in accordance with their intersubjectively acquired insights into what is in each case in the equal interest of all. Modern enforceable law assigns these two moments of the *law-abiding* and the *law-making* will to different social roles – on the one hand, to that of the private addressee of law who acts autonomously within the law as a private citizen and, on the other, to the democratic co-legislator who makes use of his or her civic autonomy. The law of modern states splits the moral person as it were into two persons, the private citizen and the national citizen.

The interaction between these two roles that every citizen fulfils in personal union provides the key for judging the liberal and social-welfare paradigms of law. These terms refer to the models of society in which the law of democratic states operates (according to the conceptions of legal practitioners). The 'private law society' of the ordoliberals, which places the weight of legitimacy in a one-sided way on the equal opportunity for private citizens to be guaranteed by economic freedoms, has experienced an unexpected rhetorical revival following the failure of neoliberal economic policies. But the welfare state model also restricts itself under aspects of distributive justice to the subjective claims of the clients of welfare bureaucracies, instead of understanding social security systems *also* as empowering their clients to participate in democratic self-legislation. In contrast, the third, procedural, paradigm of law, which I discussed in *Between Facts and Norms*, switches the focus to the self-authorization of national citizens who exercise influence collectively over their social conditions of existence. Central to this paradigm of law are the *feedback loops* between the democratic process that generates subjective rights and claims on behalf of the private citizens, as well as the safeguarding of a form of private autonomy that in turn makes it possible for national citizens to make an active use of their public autonomy. Such a form of positive feedback between private and public autonomy is a necessary condition of the legitimacy of a democratic state system. This legitimacy is jeopardized in societies with growing social divisions in which a negative class-specific feedback loop is becoming endemic. Here the rising level of abstention from elections among the marginalized and disadvantaged strata of society, on the one hand, and the privileging of policy models that neglect the interests of those segments of the population, on the other, are reinforcing each other. Empirical studies confirm the existence of such a vicious circle in the United States and in other Western societies.[3]

(5) I developed the discourse-theoretical conception of law and the democratic state at the time, taking the nation-state as my example. Since 1989/90, however, I have devoted myself for obvious political reasons to the process of European unification and the human rights policy of the United Nations. Through Kant's essay on 'Perpetual Peace' I happened upon the literature in legal studies on the constitutionalization of international law.[4] Here I can only offer some tentative reflections on what the discourse-theoretical approach could contribute to solving this problem in international law. First, I would like to explain the vantage point that seems to me to be the appropriate one for addressing this problem.

If we consider the constitutional state under discourse-theoretical aspects, then what strikes us as its major historical achievement is how it contained despotism. The egalitarian protection of freedom is, in a moral-practical sense, a civilizational achievement that can be distinguished from the mere increase in the effectiveness of the modern administrative state, of the 'rational state apparatus' in Max Weber's sense. The discourse-theoretical approach suggests conceiving of both the *advance in civilization* brought about by law and the organizational *rationalization* of the state apparatus by comparison with the ancient empires in terms of a *transformation of the substance of state power*. From this point of view, the juridification of international relations that began after the end of the Second World War with the transition from *coordinating* to *cooperative* international law, then also turns out to be a kind of continuation of this process. Since the foundation of the United Nations, of the three major global economic organizations (the World Bank, the International Monetary Fund and the World Trade Organization), and of informal negotiation systems such as the G8 and the G20, even the rudiments of a *constitutionalization of international law* have taken shape.[5] Corresponding to these changes in international law is a transformation of international relations: the constitutionalization of international law is connected with the supplementation of the powers of national governments by a growing web of international organizations that make governance beyond the nation-state possible. What appears from the perspective of legal theory as a transformation in the composition of the medium of law (6) I understand from the perspective of political science as a further *dissolution of the decisionistic substance of the power involved in the exercise of political authority* (7). However, these trends are associated for the time being with a democratic deficit (8) that could be counterbalanced only through a *transnationalization of democracy* (9). This means something different from the construction of an oversized state (10).

(6) The *constellation of law and political power* is changing in tandem with the change in the substance of state power.[6] This change is reflected in the relative weights of the components of modern law. The constitutional state, which enjoys a monopoly over the legitimate use of force, endows valid legal norms simultaneously with a legitimate and a coercive character, which is why Kant speaks in terms of 'connecting universal reciprocal coercion with the freedom of everyone'.[7] Law which is at once legitimate and coercive presents the citizens with the choice between following valid norms from personal self-interest because violation would incur sanctions or, alternatively, out of respect for the law in the light of the procedure of democratic lawmaking. But if one proceeds from the premise that a world state enjoying a monopoly over the legitimate use of force is neither possible nor desirable, a dualistic conception of an international legal system comprising both the law of peoples and the law of states seems unavoidable. On

the conventional reading, the obligatory law of states, which is enforced through the sanctioning power of the state and by courts and administrations, has a different mode of validity from and a higher level of effectiveness than international law, which is not backed up by the sanctioning power of the state. Thus, on the conventional conception, international law bases its authority on customs, international treaties and universally recognized legal principles alone, hence on the unenforced consensus of states.

Of course, this conclusion is unavoidable only as long as we assume that recognition of the legitimacy of a legal system can guarantee an average level of legal obedience only if it is backed up by the threat of coercion by the state. Today this assumption no longer holds *universally*. Existing European law provides the most advanced example of the shift in the balance between the two components of the enforceability of the law, on the one hand, and the recognition of its legitimacy and average compliance with the law, on the other. In the European Union, supranational law, insofar as it is not rejected by national constitutional courts in eligible exceptional cases, enjoys priority over the national law of the member states, even though the latter continue to exercise a monopoly over the legitimate use of force. Evidently, in European law, which has become differentiated as an independent level of regulation, the relative weights of the two components of the legal medium have shifted in favour of recognition of the legitimacy of supranational authority (of the Council and Parliament, the European Court of Justice, and the Commission).

Since the founding of the United Nations, the increase in the number of international courts, the extension of international criminal law and, above all, the rapid proliferation of international organizations in almost every possible policy field, we are also observing at least weak evidence of a similar shift between the sanctioning and legitimation components of international law. At least the gap between the sanction-backed mode of validity of state law and the soft mode of validity of international law is beginning to close as a result. Reality seems to be approaching Kelsen's unitary conception of international law, albeit at a snail's pace. In order to identify these trends as such, however, we have to view them in the light of a flexibilized concept of law. Once we modify the rigid concept of modern law accordingly, it also seems less improbable that it could one day become a routine matter to use the state monopolists over the use of legitimate force to enforce the impartial and juridically monitorable decisions of a reformed UN Security Council.

(7) Today, at the international level, there are also signs that the exercise of political authority by the state is being rationalized in ways which correspond to a change in the composition of the medium of law. The concept of state sovereignty in classical international law still presupposes a 'realist' conception of state authority (as this is understood by the school of Hans Morgenthau). Political power is supposed to manifest itself in the instrumental rationality of the self-assertion of a state that is assumed to act autonomously. Each sovereign state pursues its national interests on the international stage of competing co-players without its scope for action being in any way normatively restricted by defer-ence to the international community as a whole. This policy model of the instrumental assertion and optimi-zation of national power in the international arena finds its exaggerated legal expression in the *jus ad bellum*, the right of the sovereign state to wage wars at its own discretion, that is, without having to justify itself. As Carl Schmitt correctly recognized, the derogation of this right – that is, the prohibition of war – constituted a sea change in the history of international law. However, the fact that war is neither a legal nor the preferred means for solving international conflicts in our post-heroic age

is only the most visible sign of a rationalization of the violence at the core of political power.

The dense network of international organizations deprives classical international law of its assumed basis of power in a different way. In a highly interdependent world society, even superpowers are losing their functional autonomy in different policy fields. In view of the growing number of problems that can be solved only through joint political action, all states are finding themselves forced to cooperate. This explains the rapid increase in the number of international organizations with far-reaching regional and even global competences, and a corresponding progressive assimilation of classical foreign policy to domestic political conflicts. The decisionistic core of political power is being broken down once again in the crucible of the communicative currents of transnational negotiations and discourses. States can no longer regard themselves exclusively as sovereign, contracting subjects; on occasion they even conduct themselves as members of the international community.

(8) From the perspective of discourse theory, on the other hand, we discover the increasing democratic deficit connected with the two trends mentioned.[8] The changes in the composition of the legal medium and the exercise of political power can be explained by the intrusion of deliberative elements into the power-steered international relations of a world society undergoing economic globalization and systemic integration. But the inclusion of the citizens in supranational decision-making processes is not keeping pace with the legal domestication of the intensified cooperation among the states. On the contrary, effective governance beyond the nation-state is for the present coming at the cost of an uncompensated erosion of legitimation processes in the nation-state – even where a supranational pooling of competences, as is the case in the European Union, does

not substantially impair the constitutional controls. The improvement in the organizational functions that is being achieved at the supranational level through cooperation between states could be described as a trend towards the *rationalization* of the exercise of political power in the international arena; but we cannot qualify this trend as a *civilizing process* as long as international organizations only exercise their mandates on the basis of international treaties, hence *in forms* of law, but not yet *in accordance with democratically generated* law – that is, legitimately.

On this, consider the following simple reflection. Even when all members of an international organization are flawless democracies, the legitimation of the individual member states is increasingly insufficient to justify decisions of the organization as a whole as cooperation becomes closer and the interventions agreed upon become more invasive. From the perspective of the citizens of each of the national member states there is an asymmetry between the limited authorization of their own national representatives and the scope of the compromises borne by all of the representatives together; for these joint decisions impinge on the citizens of all of the member states indiscriminately. To this is added another deficit. In contrast to the decisions of national cabinets that cover all policy fields, the agenda of functionally specialized organizations is confined to particular areas of responsibility, so that this narrow focus does not allow the undesirable external effects of decisions to be taken into account. For both of these reasons, a certain paternalism is built into the legal basis of this kind of organized cooperation. This paternalism would not be eliminated even if, as is being proposed, international organizations could be obligated to abide by certain human rights standards.[9]

(9) I regard the fact that impotent international negotiation systems like the G8 or the G20 are even created

as a symptom that the steering capacity of existing institutions is being overtaxed by the pressing global challenges of climate change, global economic crises and imbalances, the worldwide risks of large-scale technology and so forth. The systemic constraints that are penetrating national boundaries (for example, those of the global banking sector) are quasi-natural social and economic forces that must be domesticated. A multiplication of the familiar kind of international organizations capable of coping with the increased need for regulation would, of course, merely aggravate the aforementioned legitimacy deficit. Technocratic regimes will continue to proliferate under the innocent label of 'governance' as long as sources of democratic legitimation are not successfully tapped for supranational authorities as well. A transnationalization of democracy is overdue. This project impinges on the relationship between politics and the market and meets the expected political resistance from economic liberals. However, it is also being met with scepticism by scientific observers.[10] In this respect, discourse theory may be able to help overcome the hurdles posed by concretistic mindsets.

The democratic legitimation process will be able to extend across national boundaries to a political community beyond the nation-state (such as the European Union, for example) only when it becomes possible to combine within a supranational multilevel system the three building blocks that are constitutive for every democratic system in a different way from in the nation-state.[11] Only the nation-state brings these building blocks into alignment in social space – namely, the 'national people' (as the bearer of political decision-making) with the 'state' (as the organization that enables the citizens to act collectively) and the 'legally constituted community of citizens' (as the voluntary association of free and equal individuals). The idea that *citizens and states (that are already constituted by citizens)* can participate *on an equal footing* in constituting a supranational democracy provides the stimulus for reflecting on a variable geometry of these components. The concept of 'shared sovereignty' must not be misunderstood in this context. Whereas within the framework of federal states the subnational units (such as cantons, states or 'Länder') feature only as the *constituted* components (constituted, that is, by an undivided sovereign, the people), the member states of a supranational democracy would play the role of a *constituting* power, and for this reason would retain correspondingly stronger competences within the constituted political community.

(10) The implications of this idea can be illustrated by using the example of a hypothetical extension of the European Monetary Union into a Political Union. Let us imagine a constitution-founding convention that represents the totality of the citizens of the European countries involved. Specifically, it would represent every citizen in his or her dual capacity as a directly participating citizen of a future Political Union, on the one hand, and as an indirectly participating member of one of the European peoples, on the other (where the latter have instructed their respective governments to constitute the existing nation-states as EU member states). *Because of this composition* of the constituent assembly out of European citizens and European peoples, the process of constitution-making would itself be channelled in such a way that the legitimating force of such a 'divided' popular sovereignty could be transferred from the outset only to institutions of a supranational polity beyond the nation-state.

An impediment to the formation of a federal state would be built into the constitution-founding process insofar as the representatives of the peoples would be tasked by their respective national citizens to safeguard the existence of the future member states in their role as guarantors of *a historically already realized level of freedom*. Therefore, none of the competences of the member states that are necessary for performing this role – for example, the administrative implementation of EU decisions or the monopoly over the legitimate use of force – would be up for grabs in the constitutional process itself.

This arrangement would have predictable substantive implications not just for assuring the continued existence of the member states, for the exit option they already enjoy, and for the unanimity requirement for changes to the constitution. The most important implications would concern a division of powers different from the federal pattern. Let us imagine that the convention pursued its task by way of a reform of the existing EU treaties. Then already the requirement that the right of the national constitutional courts to monitor decisions be upheld would show how the future Political Union deviated from the pattern of a European federal state. The deviation would also concern the required *equitable participation* of European citizens and the European peoples (in the guise of the member states) in the formation of a government, and also the corresponding twofold responsibility of the Commission, which would have been developed into a government, towards the European Parliament and the Council, and especially the equal participation of both institutions in all legislation. The existing decentralization of the state monopoly over the legitimate use of force and the implementation of the laws by each individual state – that is, the absence of an independent federal administrative level – would also have to be retained.

The idea of a form of sovereignty divided *at the root* would naturally only provide pointers for such a division of powers between European institutions and member states; it would leave considerable leeway for the concrete design of the state bodies and of the separation of powers at the European level. It would be a matter for argument how elements from parliamentary and presidential, as well as consociational, democracies could be combined in order to do maximum justice to European conditions under the normative aspect of an *at once democratic and workable* supranational polity.

II

European Conditions.
Continued Interventions

4

The Next Step
– An Interview[1]

HUBERT CHRISTIAN EHALT: The past forty years of European history have been extremely contradictory. The 1970s marked an opening in many respects, a strengthening of civil society, and a reappraisal of the past. The dynamization of the process of integration brought with it technocratization and economization. Can this development still be stopped?

JÜRGEN HABERMAS: It may be that these two trends that you rightly highlight are due to more general developments extending beyond Europe. The student movement of the late 1960s, viewed as a whole, triggered a phase of liberalization of our postwar societies, especially of political mentalities. In West Germany, a certain civilizing of political culture continued until the end of the 1980s at any rate. Similar trends could be discerned throughout Western Europe, though we must not forget that national histories exhibit different temporal rhythms. Since the 1980s, other liberal impulses have come from the countries of Central Europe which had liberated themselves from Soviet rule – they made the spontaneous forces of civil society into a widely influential topic. But after the reunification – which is correctly called the 'turn' [*Wende*] in Germany because it was a catch-up revolution – the tide turned. A certain triumphalism has lent momentum to the Anglo-Saxon solution to the backlog of economic problems that had built up in the meantime. In the course of the politically desired economic globalization, the Chicago School doctrine already put into practice by Reagan and Thatcher has gained worldwide acceptance. The policy of controlled inflation that was no longer sustainable had to be replaced by increased government borrowing if the welfare state was not to be destroyed by the rampant markets. At any rate, the long rhythm of rising public debt can also be seen as the reverse side of the neoliberal restriction of the room for manoeuvre of the nation-state.

CLAUS REITAN: How should the public read the texts in your books *The Crisis of the European Union* and *Europe: The Faltering Project*? As manifestos? Interventions? Visions?

HABERMAS: One can indeed call statements in the press, like this one, interventions. But manifestos? Every now and then, not very often, one signs an appeal. And visions do not belong to the remit of a professor, or among the sidelines of an intellectual. I don't want to give the impression that I could foresee the future. But maybe you have something else in mind. For me, the cynical defeatism of the so-called realist who fails to realize that the most pessimistic diagnosis does not excuse us from trying to do better is something like a structural opponent.

However, in West Germany during the Bonn era I was more provoked by the continuities in personnel, and the corresponding mentalities, extending through and beyond the Nazi period. It was only after 1989/90 that global developments directed my attention seriously to the problems of the legal and political reorganization of the world society that has been taking shape since that time. This interest was sparked during the first Iraq War by the debate over humanitarian intervention.

Since then, the constitutionalization of international law has also provided the framework for my reflections on European law and politics, though always against the background of the imbalance in the relationship between politics and the market as this is analyzed by social theory. This change in interest first found expression in 1991 in a book-length interview with Michael Haller.[2] Since the appearance of *Die postnationale Konstellation* (1998),[3] there has been a constant stream of political interventions in support of deeper European unification. The slim volume *Europe: The Faltering Project* also belongs in this context. But the essay on the Constitution for Europe, which appeared in German in 2011, is informed by a different, academic, ambition.[4] This slim volume acquired the role of an 'intervention' only in the context of the ongoing financial and banking crisis. But in essence it deals with a theoretical issue.

REITAN: Perhaps you could explain this. What led you to undertake this deeper and more detailed study of Europe – of the project of unification and the current crisis of legitimacy and economic crisis?

HABERMAS: The starting point is the economic insight that we distil from the crisis. The structural imbalances in the Eurozone call for a joint economic government that extends to other policy fields such as taxation and social welfare and leads to redistribution effects across national borders. Even now the rescue packages establish a joint-liability community, and a transfer of competences has already occurred from the national parliaments to the governments of the member states of the monetary union represented in the European Council. This de facto shift in weights alone, which will be sealed by the Fiscal Compact, forces us to make changes to the constitution if we want to prevent a further erosion of democracy in Europe. But such a step would mean a quantum leap in the unification process, at least for core Europe.

To date, European unification has been a project pursued by the elites above the heads of the populations. This went well as long as everyone benefited from it. The switchover to a project that is not merely tolerated, but is also supported, by the national populations must clear the high hurdle of founding cross-border solidarity among the citizens of Europe. This is why one should be careful not to stir up fears unnecessarily by invoking the wrong goal of a European federal state. In my essay, I try to show that a transnationalization of democracy can also assume a different form. I familiarized myself with European law to a certain extent in an attempt to answer a key question for the sceptical public: how must we conceive of the supranational polity required for closer cooperation if it is to satisfy the stringent requirements for democratic legitimacy without assuming the character of a state – and not that of the dreaded 'monster' federal state either?

REITAN: Is this why you were among the first signatories of the manifestos 'We are Europe! Manifesto for re-building Europe from the bottom up' and 'Founding Europe anew!'?

HABERMAS: Yes, the first manifesto was initiated by Ulrich Beck and Daniel Cohn-Bendit, the other by leading trade unionists and leftist economists. Despite their different approaches I found both appeals convincing. They reflect a crisis awareness that is creative rather than paralyzing. They reflect the present danger that a historical project could fail and make clear the need for a new foundation of the European Union.

EHALT: So, are we now at a point where refounding Europe in the sense of cultural curiosity about the other European nations, about the very different milieus and developments, has a chance for the first time?

HABERMAS: I am under no illusion about the scale of Euroscepticism, especially in the potential 'donor countries'. But one should not underestimate the dialectic being generated at present by the much-bemoaned economic motor of the process of unification. The business sections of the national newspapers do not really teach us about the causes of this dire situation in which the states and the European Central Bank have to allow themselves to be blackmailed into providing ever more guarantees and liquidity injections by the financial markets and an undercapitalized banking system. The states are simultaneously the clients of the banks that they have to rescue, even though the banks continue to rake in huge profits and to blithely feed the crisis as if nothing had happened. The individual governments cannot break out of this vicious circle by raising taxes, because that would deter investors and even jeopardize the remaining tax revenue from the financial sector (as in Great Britain) or from the real economy that creates values (as applies to most other European countries). The tax on financial transactions that people have been demanding for decades, which would mean that those who caused the crisis would at least have to share its costs, is being thwarted by the political disunity of Europe. And yet a cunning of economic reason is at work even in this tricky situation. This confronts us with alternatives that force us to act, even if the political elites are trying to evade such alternatives for fear of their voters. There is a lack of 'political leadership' in Europe. I am reluctant to use this expression because the unimaginative power opportunism of the political parties is normally sufficient to keep the machine running. But in times of crisis the timid and short-sighted incrementalism of small steps personified by Angela Merkel is no help.

EHALT: A number of economists, such as Joseph E. Stiglitz, are calling for a 'New Deal' for Europe instead of the ubiquitous austerity postulates.

HABERMAS: Yes, in my opinion his analyses point in the right direction. In addition, political economists like

Fritz Scharpf and Henrik Enderlein offer a rather more specific explanation for why this crisis broke out and continues to simmer in the euro currency area. The single currency has only had the effect of deepening the considerable differences in levels of development and competitiveness between the national economic systems and cultures. The mechanism of devaluing the individual national currencies that the European Monetary Union lacks cannot be counterbalanced, as in the United States, through other mechanisms – for example, cross-border labour mobility or the interregional redistribution effect of a common social policy. For this reason, in the past the euro even tended to aggravate the structural imbalances between the national economies. And that will not change as long as the slogan 'More Europe' means nothing more than an intergovernmental harmonization of the still formally independent policies of the member countries in accordance with recipes of Merkel-style austerity policy. Given the existing gap in competitiveness among the national economies, the structural differences can be brought into alignment in the medium term only through a common financial, economic and social policy that responds flexibly to the different national situations. It is not sufficient to subject all economies to the same rules. Regulatory policy is not enough. The Fiscal Compact, which only requires that the budgetary policies of the member states should observe the same rules, taken in isolation is counterproductive – we see that every day. That is why the cunning of economic reason is presenting us with the alternative between winning the support of the populations for a new political foundation of a core Europe that remains open for the accession of other EU countries – especially Poland – and allowing the euro to fail. The recent Greek elections in May 2012 have lent impetus to the idle talk of a 'Plan B'.

EHALT: Can a common Europe survive even without a common currency?

HABERMAS: There's no easy answer to that question. My knowledge of history and the political life experience of a German of my generation suggest that it would be demoralizing if the currency union were to fail for clear reasons of national egoism. Moreover, it would provide the starting signal for the right-wing populism that has undergone a revival in all of our countries. My feeling is that the European Union as a whole would then be dragged down by the failed euro. At stake at any rate is half a century of historically quite improbable achievements – the product of the visions and arduous negotiations of major politicians, not just of the three founding fathers, but also of the forward-looking perspectives of Jacques Delors, Valéry Giscard d'Estaing and Helmut Schmidt, of François Mitterrand and Helmut Kohl. Joschka Fischer was again a leading European figure for a short time. Today I cannot identify anyone anywhere in Europe who would risk a polarizing election campaign to mobilize majorities for Europe – and only that could save us. Yet the idea of Europe has long since become ingrained in the younger generations. What do you think our grandchildren would say if one day they had to show their passports once again at the national borders?

REITAN: Can citizens who have different perceptions of their two roles in the European Union – that of the members of a national state and that of citizens of the Union – nevertheless identify with both roles?

HABERMAS: The extension of national civic solidarity beyond the borders of nation-states is of course the hurdle that can condemn the now overdue task of deepening the institutions to failure. But the level of mutual trust between the European peoples that is required is also much weaker than the national consciousness that evolved historically. Even national consciousness only arose in the course of the nineteenth century – not without the energetic efforts of historians who first had to construct national histories, and not without universal conscription and the calculated influence of the press and the school system. Even civic solidarity is a pretty abstract affair, being a legally mediated form of solidarity with strangers whom one as a general rule never meets face to face. One person is willing to make certain sacrifices for another, because he or she can expect the favour to be returned sooner or later. Hasn't a sense of solidarity already developed among European citizens, as was shown on 15 February 2003, when the overwhelming majority of Western Europeans responded with one voice to the reckless war of George Bush, Jr?

REITAN: But, if we assume that people need something to hold on to, where are they more likely to find it – in their own nation-state or in a Greater Europe?

HABERMAS: That is the dilemma we are currently facing. In situations in which people are gripped by fear of downward mobility, poverty and waves of immigrants, they seek refuge in the anchor of supposedly natural national belonging. On the other hand, we would not be discussing Europe here if the same economic causes that trigger such regressions hadn't also fostered an awareness of the need to counteract the extortionate threats of the financial markets and the risks posed by banks by strengthening the scope for political action beyond the nation-state.

EHALT: Bank managers who are jointly responsible for the financial crisis receive salaries that could easily cover the cost of the salaries of all senior physicians in a large hospital. Why does the outrage remain within limits?

HABERMAS: That's a good question. For the first time in the history of capitalism, the collapse of the entire financial sector manifestly had to be averted or postponed through the guarantees of the taxpayer; and in most cases the citizens didn't even receive the corresponding property titles in return. The injustice of the burden-sharing cries out to heaven: the banks continue to gamble away merrily while the protests retain a more local character – on London streets in flames, on the Puerta del Sol in Madrid, before the City Hall in Lisbon, on Syntagma Square in Athens and so forth. Occupy Wall Street aside, these movements are as different from each other in cause, character, composition and motivation as the occasions and conditions at the national levels. The silent majorities to which these movements appeal are disheartened. They probably sense the systemic entanglements of everyone with everyone else, and are overwhelmed by the sense of the fatal impotence of their governments in the face of the potential threat of still unregulated markets. For this reason alone, we need a workable core Europe in order to re-establish a halfway tolerable balance between politics and the market.

REITAN: What would have to be done in order to make this project capable of winning majority support in a general ballot?

HABERMAS: Today the initiative rests with governments and political parties. The media have an almost equal responsibility – their task is also to criticize and prompt, after all, and not just to provide submissive commentaries. The governments and the political parties must put an end to the scandal that to date there has never been a European election or a European referendum in any member state that was not a vote on the usual national issues and national political candidates. Political parties and the media must take up an unpopular topic that they have avoided until now because it promised neither more votes nor an increase in circulation. They must provide a better definition of the project whose goal has always remained indeterminate. They could argue convincingly that 'more Europe' is also in the interests of the 'donor countries' in the medium term. But then they would have to expand the current focus on economic issues considerably. They would have to make it clear that a vote for 'more Europe' would not only signal a new foundation of the EU, but would also be a step in the direction of the democratic empowerment of European politics. Europeans can only recover their scope for political action together. It's about us, but it's also about Europe's role in the world. Given the statistically well-documented prospect that our continent will lose political influence and economic weight on a worldwide scale in proportion to its shrinking population, it is obvious that none of the European nations will have the power to uphold its social and cultural model on its own. Just as little will a decaying Europe have the strength to play a role in shaping a politically fragmented and economically stratified – and hence unjust – world society. This world society has not yet learned how to master the challenges of environmental disasters, famine and poverty, economic imbalances and the risks of large-scale technology. And a cantonized Europe that belongs in the museum – the best-case (but improbable) scenario – wants to withdraw from this planning and learning process?

5

The Dilemma Facing the Political Parties[1]

My main qualification for receiving this prize is presumably senescence. For I experienced the greater part of the nineteen-year incumbency of Georg August Zinn in Hesse first hand, and as a citizen of this state was infected by the pioneering spirit of this minister-president. At that time, the slogan 'Hesse ahead' was obvious to everyone. It was in the middle of Zinn's second term in office that I came to Frankfurt with my wife and our first, then two-month-old, child to become Adorno's assistant. I left the city and the university again only three years after the end of Georg August Zinn's fifth and final term in office.

I consider it a lucky circumstance that, back in the 1950s and 1960s, as alert contemporaries who were still young, curious and willing to learn, we experienced the most important period in postwar German history in Frankfurt and Hesse in a climate of compressed contemporaneity, as it were. The groundwork for the economic and political-institutional development had already been laid by the time we arrived. But the controversy over the orientation that the political mentality of the Federal Republic should take would be fought out most fiercely over the next fifteen to twenty years, and we found ourselves in the midst of this politically turbulent, communicatively and socially dynamic environment, in a milieu that was intellectually stimulating and irritating in equal measure. In retrospect, these were the most intense years of my adult life.

But the Hessian SPD is not honouring me because I am eighty-three years old. Reviewing the past should not deter us from examining the most pressing issue of the present day. Therefore, let us talk about Europe.

Many of us have a sense that the crisis that has been smouldering since 2008 is entering a decisive phase this autumn, because the policy of short-term stabilization of the financial markets that has been pursued until now has reached its limits. In the meantime, the politicians have also come to the realization that the single currency calls for a common fiscal, economic and social policy. For the time being, however, this is only leading to pro-European lip service. The governments are still hoping to be able to wave through the overdue economic regulations at the policy level discreetly, without having to change the political institutions. 'Even today', as the Berlin business correspondent of the *Süddeutsche Zeitung* observes, 'the governments of the euro countries have transferred a large proportion of the tasks that they should actually perform themselves to the central bank – out of naked fear that the voters would not endorse their line on the euro bailout.'[2] In view of the levels of national debt being held by the European Central Bank, it is clear that the bank, with its policy of buying up ailing government bonds, has long been following the path of a disguised 'debt union'. At the same time, this term serves in domestic politics as a bludgeon with which to marginalize any constructive proposal to deepen the Political Union – such as the recent intervention by Sigmar Gabriel. Since Herman Van Rompuy submitted a proposal for a 'genuine' fiscal and economic union to the European Council on 26 June 2012 and was charged by the heads of government to elaborate this proposal by December, the presidents of the European Council, the Commission and the European Central Bank have been busy with plans for an 'institutional solution' to the crisis. The EU Commissioner for the Internal Market and Services, Michel Barnier, has now described the long-recognized vicious circle whereby the euro countries are blackmailed by the financial markets in the following blunt terms: 'first the state helps cash-strapped banks, but public debt rises as a result, which the banks in turn buy up – which is why their situation gets even worse'.[3] Of course, the commissioner fails to mention that the private investors are the only winners in this sad game as long as the blackmail works, while the prescribed austerity policy does not lay the bill at the door of those who caused the crisis, but unapologetically at the door of the masses of already suffering citizens.

Meanwhile, ideas for a common banking supervision and a banking union designed to ease access to loans from the European Stability Mechanism (ESM) are assuming concrete form. In addition, everyone involved knows that even the resolution of the fiscal crisis in no way affects the underlying causes, namely, the structural imbalances that inevitably arise between independent national economies with different levels of competitiveness under conditions of a single currency. Observing the same budgetary rules will do nothing to counteract this in the long run either. In a noteworthy article for the German weekly *Die Zeit*, Mario Draghi goes one step further. According to Draghi, a genuine fiscal and economic union would call for a political foundation to ensure that all acted in accordance with the maxim 'that it is neither legitimate nor economically sustainable if the economic policies of individual countries entail cross-border risks for the partners in the monetary union'.[4] Draghi recognizes that 'the joint exercise of sovereign rights' necessitates a broadening of the basis of legitimacy. But that approaches the pain threshold that all governments want to avoid for the present, namely, the renewed debate over a change in the European Treaties. It is not a coincidence that the initiatives and suggestions for an institutional solution are coming from high-level officials who never have to face the voters.

If my description of the situation is correct, we are heading towards a dilemma. On the one hand, the trend towards implementing the blueprints for a true fiscal and economic union drawn up by the economic experts is being strengthened by pressure from the financial markets. In any case, the economic imperatives that have prompted the work on a new 'institutional architecture' will have to be satisfied one way or the other. However, the politicians in charge are shying away from the conclusion that follows from this. The sovereign rights that are taken away from the national parliaments in the course of the planned fiscal reconstruction would have to be transferred to a democratic legislature at the European level. They cannot be exercised by the assembled heads of government alone, because the European Council is not elected by the European citizenry as a whole. Otherwise, we violate the principle that the legislator that decides on how public money is spent must be identical with the democratically elected legislator that raises taxes for these expenditures.

I fear, however, that we would pay just this price for a technocratic resolution of the crisis. The member-state governments will concentrate the necessary powers at the European level in order to assuage 'the markets'; but at the same time they want to try to downplay the true meaning of this integration step vis-à-vis their domestic voting publics, because they can no longer count on the customary passive willingness to obey in the core countries of Europe when it comes to deepening of the Political Union. According to this scenario, we are on the post-democratic path to market-conforming executive federalism tailored to the imperatives of the financial markets. Not only would democracy fall by the wayside in the process, but we would simultaneously squander the opportunity to regulate the financial markets, even if initially only within an economic zone of continental, but not global, proportions. A European executive that becomes completely independent from a democratically mobilized electorate loses any motivation, as well as the strength, to take countermeasures.

To be sure, governments and political parties have good reasons for hesitancy. Until now, the European project has been promoted over the heads of populations by the political elites more or less alone. And the citizens were content as long as the EU was a community of winners. But now the euro crisis, which is having different effects on the national economies and is perceived in polarizing terms from the perspective of national publics, is reinforcing Eurosceptical right-wing populism everywhere. The polls show that at the moment it is not easy to win majorities for the overdue change in the Treaties. However, before we resign ourselves to accepting these moods as givens, we should first recall the normative view that political elections and ballots have a different meaning from demographic surveys.

Elections and referenda should not simply reflect a spectrum of existing preferences, but instead judgements about the programmes and the candidates for election. They should not express the will of the people in an unreflected way, because they also have a cognitive meaning. The government has to address pressing problems on the basis of such fundamental directional decisions. In a democracy, political elections do not fulfil their systemic purpose if they merely register the distribution of preferences and prejudices. Votes acquire the institutional weight of civic decisions by a co-legislator only in virtue of the fact they emerge from a process of public opinion- and will-formation steered by the public pros and cons of free-floating opinions, arguments and positions. The opinions of citizens should first *develop* out of the dissonant flood of contributions in the light of a public exchange of opinions.

Ideally, deliberative politics is rooted in a civil society that makes an anarchic use of its communicative freedoms. But our large-scale public spheres, which are a product of the communication network of the mass media, require not only the information and impulses of a spontaneous and independent press, but first and foremost the initiative, the enlightenment and the organizational capacity of political parties. In Germany, the parties have a corresponding constitutional mandate. This evening I am the guest of a political party. However, it is not a courtesy, but for you probably more an impertinence, when I say that at the moment the political fate of Europe depends primarily on the insight and the normative sensitivity, the courage, the wealth of ideas and the leadership of the political parties – though secondly, of course, also on the perceptual capabilities and responsiveness of the mainstream political media.

This is easily said in the abstract. In the first place, political parties are compelled by the tasks of acquiring and holding on to political power to tailor their planning and actions to the rhythm of legislative periods; they run additional risks and have to take responsibility for them if they relativize the importance of their pragmatic decisions to more far-reaching, historical objectives. Furthermore, they operate under the legitimacy expectations of national arenas that have hardly begun to open themselves up to each other; so political parties cannot expect any rewards if they think and act simultaneously in national and in European terms even before a European party system has come into existence. Finally, the competition between political parties at the national level restricts the room for decision-making of the coalitions that are likely candidates when it comes to alternatives in European policy. A recent example is the plight of the SPD in the German general election campaign. No party can afford to be the first to show its hand with pro-European slogans, because it has to fear a populist backlash orchestrated by its short-sighted competitors who in fact share similar goals.

Today, the political opinion- and will-formation of the general population on the momentous alternative between more and less Europe is beyond the analytical grasp of the usual commercial polls. It requires the political elites to adopt a very different, argumentative, mentality-shaping mode of politics that is capable of providing strong leadership. This is a matter of persuasion, though persuasion informed by an awareness of fallibility. One cannot reproach the political parties for being caught unprepared by this extraordinary situation. But in extraordinary situations openly acknowledging a dilemma may also be a first step towards tackling it.

6

Three Reasons for 'More Europe'[1]

I am grateful for the invitation to appear on this prominent platform as a non-lawyer. I hope that the focus of
this meeting on legal policy justifies me in supplement-
ing the discussion with reflections of a more political
nature. I also have legal questions on my mind. But to
begin with I will stick to my prepared statement.

Today economic constraints, if I may begin with a
rough thesis, present us with the alternative between
doing irreparable damage to the postwar project of
European unification by abandoning the single currency, on the one hand, and deepening the Political
Union – initially in the Eurozone – to such an extent
that transfers and the communalization of debt across
national borders can be democratically legitimized,
on the other. The one alternative cannot be avoided
without embracing the other. I would like to offer four
observations on this thesis.

(1) Let me begin with some reflections on the historical
background. Promoting the process of European integration was incumbent upon a politically and morally
compromised Germany already for prudential reasons
in order to regain the international reputation that it
had destroyed by its own actions. By embedding itself

in Europe, Germany was able to develop a liberal self-understanding for the first time. The laborious change in political mentality that took place in the old West Germany was the result of conflicts that continue to exercise effects up to the present day. On this basis, a habituation to a certain nation-state normality set in after the successful reunification (with 17 million citizens who had experienced a different political socialization). This normality is now being challenged by the crisis-charged European question. The leadership role in Europe that falls to Germany today for demographic and economic reasons is not only awakening historical ghosts all around us, but for us also represents a temptation to adopt a unilateral national course. The answer is to continue to cultivate the cautious and cooperative politics in favour of a 'Germany *in* Europe' as practised in the old West Germany.

(2) A second reason for a deeper political integration is the shift in the balance between politics and the market, which is continuing to the present day in the wake of the neoliberal self-disempowerment of politics. Politics is the only means by which democratic citizens can *intentionally* influence the fate and social bases of existence of their communities through collective action. Markets, on the other hand, are self-steered systems for decentrally coordinating a vast number of individual decisions. Viewed normatively, both media have the potential to secure freedom. In this respect, one can also understand the constitutional state as an ingenious invention that combines equal opportunities to participate in the processes through which society exercises collective influence over itself with the guarantee of equal subjective economic freedoms in such a way that the two media can enhance each other's effectiveness. A specific feature of the current crisis is the destruction of this complementarity. In the vicious circle between the profit interests of the banks and investors and the public

interest of over-indebted states, the financial markets have the upper hand. Never before have elected governments been so unceremoniously replaced by individuals with the confidence of the markets – think of Mario Monti or Loukas Papademos. While the politicians are subjugating themselves to the imperatives of the market and accept that an increase in social inequality is the price to be paid for this, systemic mechanisms are increasingly escaping the intentional influence of democratically enacted law. This trend can be reversed, if at all, only by recovering the scope for political action at the European level.

(3) A third reason connected with monetary policy for transferring further national sovereign rights to the European level follows from the necessary conditions for a single currency to function, which are not fulfilled in the Eurozone. Here I'm simply repeating arguments from another discipline. After the introduction of the euro with its uniform interest rate, the ECB was not able to compensate for the strong divergences in growth and inflation trends between the national economies. The lack of the option to devalue the currency robs the member states, whose budgetary policies remain independent, of the most important adaptive mechanism (in the shape of higher prices for imported goods). The less homogeneous the different economies are and the more their levels of competitiveness diverge, the more important are other compensatory mechanisms such as (and this does not apply to Europe) flexible wage and price adjustment, high labour mobility or – to mention the only possible mechanism in our case – transfer payments, which in the United States, for example, occur mainly through social security systems and structural programmes. There seems to be a consensus among the experts that the existing and growing structural imbalances within the Eurozone cannot be dampened without transfer payments and can be reduced, at least in the

medium term, only through common structural and economic policies. However, responsibility for political decisions with transnational redistributive effects must not be concentrated in the European Council alone, because in intergovernmental negotiation systems there is a divergence between the scopes of democratic mandates and of powers to act. The democratic legitimation of such decisions calls instead for equal participation by a legislator elected by the European citizenry as a whole, which can decide on the basis of interests *generalized across Europe* – and not according to a mode of will-formation conditioned by national self-interest like that which prevails in the European Council.

(4) These three arguments refer to longer-running developments and do not touch on the measures for mastering the present crisis. But they call to mind problems that political actors who adopt an incrementalistic approach conceal behind the veil of a noncommittal pro-European posture. The leaders present their decisions as repair work for which the national parliaments can continue to bear the brunt of legitimation. This is also how the sigh of relief of the German government following the recent judgment of the German Federal Constitutional Court must be understood. While the heads of government have their eyes on their re-election, the President of the Council, the Commission and the European Central Bank are working out an 'institutional architecture' for a 'genuine' economic and fiscal union 'based on the joint exercise of sovereignty for common policies and solidarity'.[2] To my question about the competences for such a 'joint exercise of sovereignty', Herman Van Rompuy spontaneously answered that this would call for changes not only in the European Treaties, but also in many national Constitutions. If that is what the politicians in Brussels actually think in private, then the German government is playing a clever double game.

Given this obscure situation, the judgment of the Federal Constitutional Court on 12 September 2012 acquired more than just political and operational significance. The Court should have clarified the normative basis of its decision. My impression is that, even in its previous European case law, one could not tell whether the Court was defending the nation-state for the sake of democracy or was instead defending democracy for the sake of the nation-state.[3] By adopting this defensive, sovereignty-obsessed line of argument, the Court distorted our view of the communicating vessels of national and European law. Because it assumed that the democracy clause, as formulated in Article 20 (2) of the German Basic Law, must be implemented at the national level, it had shot its bolt when it came to the competences captured by the European Council. I cannot identify in this most recent decision any constructive contribution to the transnational recovery of democracy which is under threat at the national level. At first glance, the 'yes, but' to the ESM and the Fiscal Compact, stated in the reasons for the judgment, reaffirms verbally the basic democratic norms to which the petitioners appeal. But the substance of these norms seems to evaporate in the judicial application to normatively slippery technocratic matters.

7

Democracy or Capitalism?
On the Abject Spectacle of a
Capitalistic World Society Fragmented along
National Lines

In *Buying Time*, his book on the delayed crisis of
democratic capitalism,[1] Wolfgang Streeck develops an
unsparing analysis of the origins of the present banking and debt crisis that is spilling over into the real
economy. This bold, empirically based study developed
out of Streeck's Adorno Lectures at the Institute of Social
Research in Frankfurt. In its best parts – specifically,
whenever it combines political passion with the eye-
opening force of critical factual analysis and cogent
arguments – it is reminiscent of *The Eighteenth Brumaire
of Louis Napoleon*. Its starting point is a justified critique of the crisis theory that Claus Offe and I developed
in the early 1970s. Inspired by the Keynesian optimism
concerning government regulation that was prevalent at
the time, we assumed that the economic crisis potentials
mastered by politics would be *diverted* into conflicting
demands on an overstrained governmental apparatus
and into 'cultural contradictions of capitalism' (as Daniel
Bell would put it a couple of years later), and that they
would *find expression* in a legitimation crisis. Today we
are not (yet?) experiencing a legitimation crisis, but we
are witnessing a palpable economic crisis.

The Genesis of the Crisis

Equipped with the superior knowledge of the retrospective historical observer, Wolfgang Streeck begins his account of the progress of the crisis with a sketch of the welfare state regime which was built up in postwar Europe into the early 1970s.[2] There followed the phases of the implementation of the neoliberal reforms that improved the conditions for the utilization of capital, regardless of the social costs, and in doing so tacitly inverted the meaning of the term 'reform'. In the course of these reforms, corporatist negotiation constraints were relaxed and the markets deregulated – not just the labour markets, but also the markets for goods and services, and above all the capital markets: 'The capital markets were transformed into markets for corporate control, which made of "shareholder value" the supreme maxim of good management . . .' (*Buying Time*, p. 29).

Wolfgang Streeck describes this turn, which began with Reagan and Thatcher, as the liberating blow delivered by the owners of capital and their managers against a democratic state which restricted company profit margins in favour of social justice, but which from the investors' perspective had strangled economic growth and thus had harmed the supposed public interest. The empirical material of the study consists in a longitudinal comparison between relevant countries over the past four decades. Notwithstanding the differences between the national economies, the picture that emerges is that the general progress of the crisis has been astonishingly uniform. The rising rates of inflation of the 1970s were replaced by increases in public and private household debt. At the same time, the inequality in the distribution of income and wealth increased, while public revenues decreased relative to public expenditures. With growing social inequality, this development led to a transformation of the tax state:

'The democratic state, ruled and (qua tax state) resourced by its citizens, becomes a democratic debt state as soon as its subsistence depends not only on the financial contributions of its citizens but, to a significant degree, on the confidence of its creditors' (p. 80).

The perverse consequences of the restriction of the state's political decision-making power by 'the markets' can be observed in the European Monetary Union. Here the transformation of the tax state into a debt state provides the backdrop for the vicious circle between ailing banks being rescued by states and these states in turn being driven to ruin by these same banks – with the result that the population have been reduced to wards of the reigning financial regime. What this means for democracy could be observed under the microscope during the summit in Cannes at which Greek Prime Minister Papandreou was forced by his backslapping colleagues to cancel a planned referendum.[3] Wolfgang Streeck is to be commended for demonstrating that the 'politics of the debt state' that has been pursued by the European Council since 2008 at the urging of the German government is essentially a continuation of the capital-friendly policy model that led to the crisis in the first place.

Under the specific conditions of the European Monetary Union, the policy of fiscal consolidation is subjecting all member states to the same rules regardless of the differences between their levels of economic development, and, in order to enforce these rules, is concentrating rights of intervention and control at the European level. Without a simultaneous strengthening of the European Parliament, this concentration of competences in the Council and the Commission is ensuring that the national public arenas and parliaments are becoming uncoupled from the aloof, technocratically self-propelling concert of governments beholden to the markets. Wolfgang Streeck is afraid that pushing through executive federalism in this way will lead to a completely new way of exercising political authority in Europe:

> The consolidation of government finances as an answer to the fiscal crisis comes down to a remodelling of the European state system coordinated by financial investors and the European Union – a reconstitution of capitalist democracy in Europe with the purpose of enshrining the results of three decades of economic liberalization. (p. 117)

This extreme interpretation of the ongoing reforms captures an alarming trend that will probably prevail, even though it revokes the historical connection between democracy and capitalism. The gates of the European Monetary Union are being guarded by a British prime minister for whom the neoliberal phase-out of the welfare state cannot happen quickly enough, and who, as the true heir of Margaret Thatcher, cheerfully goads a willing German Chancellor into wielding the whip among her colleagues: 'We want a Europe that wakes up to this modern world of competition and flexibility.'[4] There are two alternatives – in theory – to this crisis policy: either the defensive option of winding down of the euro, to which end a new party has recently been founded in Germany,[5] or the offensive option of extending the monetary union into a supranational democracy. The latter alternative, assuming corresponding political majorities, could provide the institutional platform for reversing the neoliberal trend.

The Nostalgic Option

It is no surprise that Wolfgang Streeck opts for reversing the trend towards de-democratization. This means 'building institutions through which markets can be brought back under the control of society: labour markets that leave scope for social life, product markets that do not destroy nature, credit markets that do not mass-produce unsustainable promises' (p. 174). But the concrete conclusion that he draws from this diagnosis is all the more surprising. His conclusion is not that the Union stuck in midstream should be extended in a democratic way in order to bring the disjointed relationship between politics and the market back into an equilibrium compatible with democracy. Instead of expansion, Wolfgang Streeck recommends dismantling. He favours a return to the defensive nation-state constellation of the 1960s and 1970s so as 'to defend and repair what is left of the institutions with whose help social justice might be able to modify or even replace market justice' (p. 174).

It is surprising that Streeck chooses this nostalgic option of retreating into the sovereign impotence of the overrun nation when we consider the epoch-making transformation that nation-states have undergone – from states that still exercised control over their territorial markets into disempowered co-players embedded in globalized markets. The need for political governance to which the highly interdependent world society is giving rise is at best being cushioned by an increasingly dense network of international organizations. But the asymmetrical relations of the much-vaunted 'governance beyond the nation-state' are no match for this problem. In view of the pressure being generated by the problems of a world society that is becoming integrated at the systemic level while remaining anarchic at the political level, the initial reaction to the outbreak of the global financial crisis in 2008 was understandable. The aghast governments of the G8 countries responded by hastening to include the BRIC states and a couple of other countries in their consultations. On the other hand, the ineffectuality of the resolutions taken at the first G20 conference in London documents the defect that would only be exacerbated by restoring the breached national bastions – the political fragmentation of a nevertheless economically integrated world society would undermine the ability to cooperate.

Evidently, the political decision-making power of nation-states that jealously guard their long-since hollowed-out sovereignty is not sufficient to escape the grip of the imperatives of a colossally bloated and dysfunctional banking sector. States that do not unite to form supranational units, and have to rely on international treaties alone, fail when faced with the political challenge of reconnecting the banking sector with the needs of the real economy and reducing it to the functionally required scale. The states in the European Monetary Union are confronted in a special way with the task of bringing irreversibly globalized markets within the ambit of indirect but well-aimed political influence. In fact, however, their crisis policy is limited to expanding an expertocracy for temporizing measures. Without the pressure exerted by the will-formation of a vital civil society that can be mobilized across national borders, a self-propelling Brussels executive lacks the strength and the motivation to re-regulate untamed markets in socially sustainable ways.

Wolfgang Streeck is of course aware that 'the power of investors feeds mainly on their advanced international integration and the presence of efficient global capital markets' (p. 88). Looking back on the global victory march of deregulation policy, he emphasizes that he has to 'leave it open whether and how, in an increasingly international economy, nationally organized democratic politics could have successfully brought such developments under control' (p. 75). He repeatedly emphasizes the 'organizational advantage that globally integrated financial markets have over nationally organized societies' (p. 86). Hence, one might think that his own analysis would force him to conclude that the power of democratic legislation to regulate markets, which was at one time concentrated in the nation-states, should be restored at the supranational level. In spite of this, he sounds the retreat behind the Maginot Line of national sovereignty.

However, at the end of the book he flirts with the aimless aggression of self-destructive resistance that has abandoned all hope of a constructive solution.[6] This betrays a certain scepticism concerning his own call to consolidate what remains of the national heritage. In the light of this resignation, his proposal for a 'European Bretton Woods' (p. 185ff.) seems like an afterthought. The profound pessimism in which the narrative ends raises the question of the implications of his plausible diagnosis that capitalism and democracy are drifting apart for the prospects of a change in policy. Does it betray a fundamental incompatibility of democracy and capitalism? In order to answer this question, we have to get clear on the theoretical background of the analysis.

Democracy or Capitalism?

The *framework* for the crisis narrative is an interaction involving three players: the state, which is funded by taxes and is legitimized by votes; the economy, which must cater for capitalist growth and a sufficient level of tax revenue; and, finally, the citizens who lend the state their political support only if it satisfies their interests in return. The *theme* is provided by the question of whether and, if so, how the state manages to strike a balance between the conflicting demands of the two sides through intelligent crisis prevention. On pain of suffering economic crises or crises of social disintegration, the state, on the one hand, has to accommodate the profit expectations of companies by guaranteeing the fiscal, legal and infrastructural conditions for a profitable utilization of capital; on the other hand, it must ensure equal freedoms for all and redeem calls for social justice in the currency of fair income distribution and status security, as well as of public services and the provision of collective goods. The *content* of the narrative is that the neoliberal strategy accords the satisfaction of capital valorization interests priority in principle over demands for social justice, and can 'delay' crises only at the cost of growing social unrest.[7]

Does the 'delayed crisis of democratic capitalism' announced in the title of the book suggest that an inevitable crisis is only being delayed or that it can be deferred indefinitely (so to speak *ad calendas graecas*)? Because Wolfgang Streeck develops his scenario within the framework of a theory of action without relying on 'laws' of the economic system (for example, a 'tendency of the rate of profit to fall'), his account is wisely not structured in such a way that it implies any theoretically supported prediction. Within this framework, only evaluations of historical conditions and contingent constellations of power yield predictions about the further course of the crisis. However, Wolfgang Streeck lends his account of the crisis tendencies a certain rhetorical air of inevitability by rejecting the conservative thesis of the 'inflationary demands of mischievous masses' and situating the crisis dynamic squarely on the side of capitalist commercial interests. The political initiative has in fact come from this side since the 1980s. But I cannot detect in this a sufficient reason for a defeatist abandonment of the European project.

I have the impression that Wolfgang Streeck underestimates the ratchet effect not only of legally *valid* constitutional norms, but also of the *actually existing* democratic complex – the forces of inertia of the established institutions, rules and practices embedded in political cultures. An example of this is provided by

the mass protests in Lisbon and elsewhere that induced
Portuguese President Aníbal Cavaco Silva to initiate a
review procedure against the social scandal of the austerity policy of his fellow party members in government.
As a result, the Portuguese constitutional court annulled
parts of the corresponding international Treaty between
Portugal and the European Union and the International
Monetary Fund, and led the government to reconsider
at least for a brief moment implementing the 'dictate of
the markets'.

The Ackermannian shareholder expectations concerning returns on investments[8] are no more facts of
nature than are the elitist notions, nourished by a servile
press, of a spoiled, internationally aloof managerial
class who treat 'their' politicians like incompetent servants. The way the Cyprus crisis was handled when it
was no longer a matter of rescuing each country's own
banks suddenly revealed that those who had caused the
crisis could indeed be called to account instead of the
taxpayers. State budgets encumbered with debts could
just as well be brought back into line through increases
in revenues as through cuts in expenditures. However,
a necessary presupposition for possibly eliminating
the structural defect of a suboptimal monetary union
would be realized only by an institutional framework
for a joint European fiscal, economic and social policy.
Only a joint European effort, not the abstract unreasonable requirement that each country should improve its
national competitiveness through its own efforts, can
promote progress towards the overdue modernization
of outmoded economic and clientelistic administrative
structures.

Two innovations above all would differentiate a
democratic version of the European Union, which
for obvious reasons could initially include only the
members of the European Monetary Union, from
market-conforming executive federalism: *first*, joint

political framework planning, corresponding transfer payments and reciprocal liability of the member states; and, *second*, the revisions of the Treaty of Lisbon that are required in order to democratically legitimize the corresponding competences, in particular equal involvement by Parliament and Council in the lawmaking process and equal accountability of the Commission to both institutions. In that case, political decision-making would no longer depend exclusively on dogged compromises fought out between representatives of national interests who block each other, but would depend equally on majority decisions of the deputies elected in accordance with party preferences. A generalization of interests *that cuts across national borders* is only possible in a European Parliament organized into parliamentary factions. A generalized We-perspective of the EU citizens throughout Europe can solidify into institutionalized power only in the parliamentary process. Such a change in perspective is necessary if the rule-bound coordination of pseudo-sovereign single-state policies favoured until now is to be replaced by joint discretionary decision-making in the relevant policy fields. The unavoidable effects of short- or medium-term redistribution can be legitimized only if national interests become aligned with the European general interest and also relativize themselves in relation to it.

Whether and how majorities could be won for a corresponding revision of the primary legislation of the EU is a question, moreover a very difficult one, to which I will return briefly below. But quite apart from whether a reform is feasible under present circumstances, Wolfgang Streeck doubts whether the format of a supranational democracy even fits with the conditions in Europe. He questions the viability of such a political system and does not think that it is desirable either, because of its supposedly repressive character. But are the four reasons he cites in support of this also good reasons?[9]

Reasons against a Political Union

The *first* and comparatively *strongest argument* is directed against the effectiveness of regional economic programmes given the historical heterogeneity of business cultures that we must take as a given also in core Europe. In fact, the policy of a monetary union must be geared to reducing, or at least curbing, structural disparities in competitiveness between the national economies in the long run. As counter-examples, Wolfgang Streeck cites the former East Germany since the reunification and the Mezzogiorno. These two cases undoubtedly call to mind the sobering, medium-term timescales that always have to be reckoned with when it comes to the targeted promotion of economic growth in backward regions. For the regulative problems that a European economic government will have to contend with, however, the two examples cited are too untypical to justify pessimism in principle. The reconstruction of the East German economy involves the historically entirely new problem of an 'assimilating' system change, one not undertaken by the system itself but steered by West German elites, within a nation that was divided for four decades. The relatively large transfer payments do seem to be having the desired effect in the medium term.

The situation is different in the case of the more stubborn problems posed by the economic stimulation of the backward and impoverished south of Italy. This region exhibits premodern social and cultural traits alien to the state, and is politically debilitated by the Mafia. Because of its special historical background, this example is not especially informative either when it comes to the anxiety currently expressed by Northern Europe concerning certain Southern European countries. The problem of the division within Italy is bound up with the long-term effects of the national unification of a country that has lived under changing foreign regimes since the end of the Roman Empire. The historical roots of the present-day problem can be traced back to the failed Risorgimento, which was conducted as a military campaign by the House of Savoy and was experienced as usurpation by the South. The more or less unsuccessful efforts of postwar Italian governments must also be seen within this context. As Streeck himself observes, these efforts became ensnared in the corrupt relations between the governing parties and local power structures. The political implementation of the development programmes was thwarted by a corruption-prone administration and not by the resistance of a social and economic culture that drew its strength from a form of life worthy of preservation. In the context of the legally highly codified European multilevel system, however, the rocky administrative road from Rome to Calabria and Sicily is not a credible model for the national implementation of programmes originating in Brussels, in whose realization sixteen other wary nations would be involved.

The *second argument* refers to the fragile social integration of 'imperfect nation-states' like Belgium and Spain (p. 179). Referring to the festering conflicts between Walloons and Flemings, and between Catalonia and the central government in Madrid, Wolfgang Streeck draws attention to integration problems that, in view of regional diversity, are already difficult to master within a nation-state – and how much more difficult would it be to cope with them in a Greater Europe! Granted, the complex state-formation process did in fact leave behind unresolved lines of conflict with older formations. We need only think of the Bavarians who rejected the German Basic Law in 1949, the peaceful separation of Slovakia from the Czech Republic, the bloody disintegration of Yugoslavia, Basque and Scottish separatism, the Northern League and so forth. But conflicts arise along these historical fault lines whenever the most vulnerable sections of the population become caught up in disruptive economic crises or historical upheavals and process their fear of a loss of status by clinging to supposedly 'natural' identities, whether it be the 'tribe', region, language or nation that promises to provide this supposedly natural basis of identity. The resurgence of nationalism that was to be expected in the Central and Eastern European countries following the collapse of the Soviet Union is in this respect a social-psychological equivalent of the separatism occurring in the 'old' national states.

The supposedly 'organic' character of these identities is equally fictive in both cases.[10] It is not a historical fact from which an obstacle to integration could be deduced. Regression phenomena of this kind are symptoms of a failure of political and economic systems that have ceased to generate sufficient levels of social security. The sociocultural diversity of the regions and nations is a valuable heritage that sets Europe apart from other continents, not a barrier that restricts Europe to a small-state mode of political integration.

The first two objections address the viability and stability of a closer Political Union. With a *third argument*, Wolfgang Streeck also wants to question its desirability: a politically enforced assimilation of the economic cultures of the South to those of the North would also mean a levelling of the corresponding forms of life. One might speak of an enforced homogenization of conditions of social life in the case of a 'grafting of a uniform economic and social model' (p. 175) inspired by radical market-oriented policies. But the difference between democratic and market-conforming decision-making processes must not be blurred in this respect in particular. The democratically legitimized decisions

taken at the European level on regional economic programmes or country-specific measures to rationalize
public administrations would also result in a standardi-
zation of social structures. But to expose all politically
promoted modernization to the suspicion of enforced
homogenization would be to make a communitarian
fetish out of family resemblances between economic
systems and forms of life. Besides, the worldwide dif-
fusion of similar social infrastructures that is at present
transforming almost all societies into 'modern' societies
is everywhere triggering individualization processes and
a proliferation of forms of life.[11]

No European 'Volk'?

Finally, Wolfgang Streeck shares the assumption that
the egalitarian ethos of constitutional democracy can
be realized only if it is based on national solidarity, and
thus only within the territorial limits of a nation-state,
because otherwise minority cultures would inevitably be
outvoted. Quite apart from the extensive discussion on
cultural rights, this assumption is arbitrary when viewed
from a long-term perspective. Nation-states already rest
on the highly artificial form of solidarity among strangers that was first produced by the legally constructed
status of citizenship. Even in ethnically and linguisti-
cally homogeneous societies, national consciousness is
not a natural phenomenon but an administratively promoted product of historiography, the media, universal
conscription and so forth. The case of national consciousness in heterogeneous immigrant societies shows
that any population can assume the role of a 'political
nation' that is capable of forming a common political
will against the background of a shared political culture.

Because classical international law stands in a complementary relation to the modern system of states, a

similarly profound metamorphosis of the nation-state is reflected in the radical innovations in international law since the end of the Second World War. The room for manoeuvre of popular sovereignty has shrunk together with the actual substance of formally guaranteed state sovereignty. This is especially true of the European states that have transferred part of their sovereign rights to the European Union. Although their governments still regard themselves as 'sovereign subjects of Treaties', even the qualification of the right to secede from the Union (introduced in the Lisbon Treaty) betrays a restriction of their sovereignty. This is in any case becoming a fiction because of the functionally grounded priority of European law. The national legal systems are becoming progressively more intermeshed at the horizontal level as legislation enacted at the European level is implemented. This renders the question of the sufficient democratic legitimization of this lawmaking all the more urgent.

Wolfgang Streeck is wary of the 'unitarian-Jacobin' traits of supranational democracy, because it would also inevitably lead to a levelling of 'identities and spatially based communities' (p. 179) through a permanent outvoting of minorities. In so arguing, he underestimates the innovative, creative legal imagination that has already found expression in the existing institutions and applicable regulations. I have in mind the ingenious 'double majority' decision-making procedure or the weighted composition of the European Parliament which makes allowances for the sharp differences in size of population between smaller and larger member states, specifically for reasons of fair representation.[12]

Above all, however, Streeck's fear of a repressive centralization of competences is nourished by the false assumption that the institutional deepening of the European Union would inevitably lead to a kind of European federal republic. The federal state is the

wrong model. A supranational, but *trans-state*, democratic political community that permits *joint governance*
also satisfies the conditions of democratic legitimation.
In such a political community, all political decisions are
legitimized by the citizens *in their dual role* as European
citizens, on the one hand, and as citizens of their respective national member states, on the other.[13] In such a
Political Union, which must be clearly distinguished
from a 'superstate', the member states, as the guarantors of the level of law and freedom embodied in them,
would preserve their very strong status compared to the
subnational components of a federal state.

What Now?

As long as it remains abstract, however, all that a well-
reasoned political alternative has going for it is its power
to develop a perspective – it points to a political goal but
does not reveal the path that leads to it. The manifest
obstacles along this path tend to support a pessimistic
assessment of the viability of the European project. It is
the combination of two facts that must worry the proponents of 'More Europe'.

On the one hand, the consolidation policy (on the
model of 'debt brakes') aims to establish a European
economic constitution that lays down 'the same rules
for all' and is supposed to remain beyond the reach
of democratic will-formation. By uncoupling technocratic orientations with momentous implications for the
European citizenry as a whole in this way from opinion-
and will-formation in the national public arenas and
parliaments, it devalues the political resources of these
citizens who only have access to their national arenas.
As a result, European policy makes itself increasingly
unassailable. This trend towards self-immunization is
being reinforced, on the other hand, by the disastrous

fact that maintaining the fiction of the fiscal sovereignty of the member states is steering public perceptions of crisis in the wrong direction. The pressure being exerted by the financial markets on the politically fragmented national budgets fosters a collectivizing self-perception of the populations affected by the crisis. The crisis is turning the 'donor' and the 'beneficiary countries' against each other and is fomenting nationalism.

Wolfgang Streeck draws attention to this demagogic potential: 'In the rhetoric of international debt politics, nations appear as monistically conceived, integral moral actors with joint liability. Domestic class and power relations are not taken into consideration' (p. 92) (translation amended). In this way, a crisis policy whose constitutional status immunizes it against critical voices and the distorted mutual perceptions of the 'peoples' in national public arenas reinforce each other.

This impasse can be overcome only if pro-European parties conduct joint transnational campaigns against this falsifying representation of social questions as national questions. I think the statement that '[i]n Western Europe today the greatest danger is not nationalism, least of all German nationalism' (p. 189) is politically foolish. The only reason I can think of for why our national public arenas are free of controversies over properly conceived political alternatives is that the democratic parties are afraid of the potential of the political Right. Controversies over the course to be pursued in core Europe will have clarifying, and not just inflammatory and polarizing, effects only if all sides concede that there are no alternatives without risks or costs.[14] Instead of opening up false fronts along national lines, the task of political parties and trade unions would be to differentiate between the winners and losers of the crisis management according to social groups who are encumbered to greater or lesser extents, *independently of their nationality*.

The European parties on the Left are set to repeat their historical error of 1914. They too are folding out of fear of a social mainstream susceptible to right-wing populism. Moreover, in Germany, an unspeakable media landscape of Merkel devotees is reinforcing all those involved in their resolve not to touch the hot potato of European policy in the election campaign and to play along with Merkel's cleverly malign game of suppressing the issue. This is why we should wish the 'Alternative für Deutschland' success. I hope that it forces the other parties to show their hand when it comes to European policy. Then, after the German general election, it might be possible to form a 'grand' coalition for the overdue first step. For, as things stand, Germany alone is in a position to take the initiative in realizing such a difficult enterprise.

III

German Jews,
Germans and Jews

8

Jewish Philosophers and Sociologists as Returnees in the Early Federal Republic of Germany

A Recollection[1]

I cannot make a contribution to exile research on the present occasion. Instead I must confine myself to sifting through some recollections from the unreliable perspective of a contemporary witness. After their return to the homeland that had expelled them, Jewish émigrés became irreplaceable teachers for a younger generation. Gershom Scholem's painful observation that the so-called 'German-Jewish symbiosis' had been a *mésalliance* from the beginning holds true for sociology and politics; it throws light on an asymmetry in the exchanges between the two sides that has been repeatedly denied. My present words also represent a continuation of such an asymmetry. For I am speaking from the perspective of a beneficiary without going into the experiences of the returnees themselves, who had to find their feet in a climate marked in part by hostile resentment and in part by an embarrassed-communicative hushing up of the mass murder that had been committed just a few years earlier.[2]

However, Jews have exhibited such an incomparable creativity in German philosophy since the days of Moses Mendelssohn that the proportional contributions of both sides to the shared objective mind are inseparably fused. Ernst Cassirer drew upon German sources of the European Enlightenment when defending the rational legal foundations of Weimar democracy against their despisers on 11 August 1928 on the occasion of the constitutional celebration, just as when, a short time later, he engaged in his major controversy with the then already anti-humanist Heidegger in Davos in March 1929. Thus, the Jewish background of authors such as Husserl, Simmel, Scheler or Cassirer did not necessarily represent a *philosophically* relevant difference for a student who had come to the university in 1949 with a reasonably clear sense of the historical significance of Auschwitz.

What made a difference for us at the time was the divisiveness of the political fates of those banished philosophers who returned. The perception of the fates of Karl Löwith or Helmuth Plessner as émigrés, whose books we read at the philosophy department in Bonn alongside those of Hans Freyer and Arnold Gehlen, is the key to understanding the outstanding importance that Jewish philosophers acquired in the old Federal Republic for the education of some members of my generation and many members of the following generation. The breakdown in civilization had made us suspicious of what was specifically German in the depths – or better, the shallows – of German traditions. One thing at least was intuitively clear to us: who if not those who had been 'racially discarded' while their colleagues blithely continued as before, who else could have developed a sharper sensibility for the dark elements in the best of our morally corrupt traditions?

The Few Who Returned

Most of the émigrés decided to return, if at all, during the first years of the newly founded Federal Republic. Very few of them received appointments. Between 1949 and 1953, the philosophers Theodor W. Adorno, Max Horkheimer, Helmut Kuhn, Michael Landmann, Karl Löwith and Helmuth Plessner returned from exile to Frankfurt, Erlangen or Munich, Berlin, Heidelberg and Göttingen. Among them, above all, Karl Löwith and Helmuth Plessner exercised an influence that extended beyond their immediate workplace. Löwith's critique of ideas in the philosophy of history, inspired by the history of salvation, may also have confirmed some of the war veterans among the students in rejecting the ideas of 1789; but reading *Weltgeschichte und Heilsgeschehen* (*Meaning in History*) aroused in all students above all a salutary distrust of the use of background assumptions of the philosophy of history as a substitute for metaphysics. His other major work, *From Hegel to Nietzsche*, still reflects the younger Löwith's interests in the *individual in the role of a fellow human being*. It made such an impression on me that I subsequently added an introductory chapter on the Young Hegelians to my dissertation after I had completed the main part.

Before the emigration, Helmuth Plessner had been one of the founders of philosophical anthropology along with Max Scheler; for us students the relevance of Plessner's older works, especially *Die Stufen des Organischen und der Mensch* as well as the study on *Laughing and Crying*, remained undiminished. With his idea of 'eccentric positionality', he opposed to Gehlen's authoritarian institutionalism a concept of human beings geared to the civilizing process, to reciprocal concern and tact. In the shadowy domain of the early Adenauer period, Plessner's *Die Verspätete Nation*, indeed all of his political-historical works, had something liberating.

Characteristically, it was the liberal left-Catholic journal, *Frankfurter Hefte*, which invited me to review these writings.

Ernst Bloch, who had already returned to Leipzig in 1949, is a special case, though if I remember correctly, he did not play any appreciable role in the discussions in the early Federal Republic. The author of what was by then a forgotten book, *The Spirit of Utopia*, became a literary presence for us again only with the publication of *The Principle of Hope*. Incidentally, Siegfried Unseld[3] revered none of his 'academic' authors as much as he did Bloch. The rhapsodic works found a wider audience only in the course of the student movement. In retrospect, one might say that Bloch's expressionistic Marxism survives as an idiosyncratic document of the time and in the history of literature, but one that left too few lasting traces within the profession.

The émigrés mentioned had all taught at German or German-speaking universities before 1933. However, their return did not always run smoothly. For example, the sociologists Julius Kraft, Gottfried Salomon-Delatour and Alphons Silbermann were able to resume teaching at the Universities of Frankfurt and Cologne only in 1957 and 1958 in the course of the 'restitution'. The sociologist and Mannheim student Norbert Elias taught in Leicester and at the University of Ghana in Accra, and settled in Amsterdam after his retirement in 1975. From there, it was not until the age of seventy-nine that he found an enthusiastic following – and at the same time also an enthusiastic reception beyond the boundaries of his academic field – with the publication in 1976 of the paperback edition of his main work *The Civilizing Process* from the 1930s.[4] The economist and social theorist Alfred Sohn-Rethel, who became a professor in Bremen in 1978, hence only at the age of seventy-nine, and the philosopher Ulrich Sonnemann, who was appointed to a professorship in Kassel in 1974, remained academic outsiders. Both became cult authors on campus at the time. Günther Anders, son of the well-known developmental psychologist William Stern and one-time husband of Hannah Arendt, was originally a philosopher. He had done his doctorate under Husserl and had already returned to Vienna in 1950, but without being able to regain a foothold in the German-speaking universities. However, for a while he enjoyed major journalistic success as a philosophical essayist and a critical commentator on contemporary developments, especially with his philosophical-anthropological reflections on the 'atomic age'.

The Return of the Non-Returnees

Thus relatively few philosophers returned at all. Viewed from the perspective of their historical impact, the intellectual influence of the émigrés who did not return in person was sometimes even greater. The durability of the posthumous influence of Ludwig Wittgenstein, who died in 1951 and immediately achieved worldwide philosophical renown with his *Philosophical Investigations*, is comparable in breadth only to the very different, literary and public impact of Walter Benjamin. Benjamin had fallen into oblivion in postwar Germany. The fate of this missing person is an exemplary gauge of the deadly violence of an exile that can expunge all traces of a figure from the cultural memory of a nation. In no other case have the opacity and the exalted character of an unsettled biography, and the tragic irony of a voluntary-involuntary death on the threshold of freedom, transferred so directly from the genesis of a work to the history of its reception.

Wolfgang Stegmüller, more than anyone else, successfully continued the tradition of the Vienna Circle within the profession. At that time, logical empiricism also dominated the most important American philosophy departments. Alongside Rudolf Carnap and Carl Gustav Hempel, reading Alfred Tarski, Herbert Feigl, Otto Neurath, Friedrich Waismann and Victor Kraft was also a must until well into the 1960s for those of us who had not received this philosophical diet as a birthright. In contrast, Hans Reichenbach, who died prematurely in 1953, became influential in postwar Germany only, if I am not mistaken, through the work of his pupil Hilary Putnam. The work of Karl Popper achieved outstanding importance ultimately thanks to the mediation of Hans Alberts. Popper's *Logik der Forschung* from 1934 (published in a revised English version, *The Logic of Scientific Discovery*, in 1959) became important for the social sciences in particular, where it continues to play a central role in methodological debates.

As influential mavericks, I would like to mention, finally, Hannah Arendt, Hans Jonas, Leo Strauss and Gershom Scholem.

Hannah Arendt also came to prominence in the United States as a philosopher only in 1958 with her book *The Human Condition*. I am indebted to this book, especially its model of the Greek public sphere, for essential stimuli for *Structural Transformation of the Public Sphere*, which I was working on at the time. The reading of this book was also important for me for another reason: it provided me with a twofold rebuttal of an academic prejudice that my teacher Erich Rothacker had repeated in his seminar in the early 1950s, according to which 'Jews and women' supposedly can only amount to 'second-rate starlets' in philosophy. Hannah Arendt generated wide attention in the Federal Republic during the student movement and afterwards. What interested her in this revolt was less the spectrum of leftist goals than the mode of the movement itself – it was politics through the agency of communicative action that fascinated her. Today her political philosophy is a fixed part of the curriculum.

Unfortunately, Hans Jonas's sophisticated philosophical works have only received a selective reception in Germany. Jonas enjoyed a belated success during the environmental movement with his book *The Imperative of Responsibility*. His early work on Gnosticism was taken up appreciatively in the theological discussion; however, his works on philosophical anthropology still await a productive reception that develops them further.

The political philosophy of Leo Strauss, which seems to have had an impact on a large number of productive students in the United States through his influence as an imposing academic teacher, has not enjoyed a comparable reception in Germany. Strauss revived classical natural law through impassioned readings and set it in opposition to modern rational law. In Germany, however, apart from a notable exception such as Wilhelm Hennis, who made the rehabilitation of natural law fruitful for his theory of government, Strauss even during his lifetime enjoyed the status of a respected but little-used classic. That could change with Heinrich Meier's commendable edition of Strauss's works[5] and with studies in the history of ideas on the situation of the author Strauss within the intellectual network of the Weimar period.

Gershom Scholem was active in Germany as the actual executor of his friend Walter Benjamin. But not only his interpretations of Benjamin and his positions on the politics of history, and not only his own scholarly lifework on Jewish mysticism, made him into the sole figure to highlight the genuinely Jewish element in the destiny and cultural productivity of the German Jews. He also embodied this element impressively in his person – and in the immaculate prose of his memoirs. Scholem enjoyed the authority of the 'Jewish Jew'. For me, the reading of *Major Trends in Jewish Mysticism* contained a big surprise. It made me aware for the first time of the amazing parallels between the thought and imagery of the Protestant mysticism of Jacob Boehme, on the one hand, and the Jewish Kabbalah of Isaac Luria, who died in Safed in 1572, on the other.

Influence within Academe

This list of names still does not provide any picture of the dynamics of the unprecedented impact of Jewish voices in an unsettled and sheepish university milieu and in the public sphere, which was marked in the early Federal Republic by an aggressively ahistorical determination to rebuild and a rock-hard anti-communist mindset that served to repress the traumatic breakdown in civilization. I will offer some select remarks first on the academic and then on the public influence of the returned émigrés. As regards conditions within the university, take my orientation roughly from 'schools' which, unlike the present day, were still clearly discernible in subjects like philosophy and sociology during the first postwar decades.

Towards the end of the 1950s, three traditional currents of unequal weights were taking shape in philosophy. The broad current of phenomenology and hermeneutics that continued to flow through the Nazi period remained decisive for the organization of the expert community and the recruitment of young talent. A major continuity in personnel persisted in this reservoir; here the self-conscious adaptation of former Nazis and fellow travellers was no less depressing than in most of the other disciplines. The politically largely unencumbered Hans-Georg Gadamer, whom the Russians had installed in Leipzig as the first rector, stood for a liberal opening of this camp, which was in any case heterogeneous. He brought his friend Karl Löwith back from exile and, together with another returned émigré, Helmut Kuhn, edited the *Philosophische Rundschau*, at the time the leading professional journal. There were two other, very unequal, competing currents: on the one hand, Critical Theory – a variant of Hegelian Marxism developed further in the 1920s with the help of Max Weber's sociology of bureaucracy – and, on the other, analytical philosophy of science. Jewish émigrés were representative figures in both schools, but initially without major influence within the profession.

Critical Theory was basically focused on the Frankfurt Institute of Social Research, in the final analysis on the person of Adorno. Adorno's first official appearance before the community of experts at the Seventh German Congress of Philosophy in 1962 in Münster was instructive concerning the low standing of this faction. The two keynote addresses on the theme of the conference, 'Philosophy and the Question of Progress', were held by Adorno and Löwith, two Jewish scholars. What was noteworthy was not that the two speakers, as expected, presented contrapuntal variations on the theme, with the one speaking on 'Das Verhängnis des Fortschritts' ('The Disaster of Progress'), while the other spoke of 'progress' in a straightforwardly affirmative sense. What was noteworthy was the style that set Adorno the intellectual apart from the assembled guild – the literary ambition of the text he delivered and his unconventional presentation provoked irritation. After finishing his lecture, Adorno bowed a shade too deeply, like a virtuoso before his public; nothing could have revealed more painfully his strangeness among his professorial colleagues.

This isolation also reflects the gulf between the university and the stage of the media public that still existed at the time. For this was the stage on which Adorno reached a broad educated public, but especially high-school teachers, students and pupils, through channels that are quite old-fashioned by today's standards (namely, radio lectures and articles in the *Frankfurter Allgemeine Zeitung* and *Merkur*, and shortly afterwards also publications in edition suhrkamp). From the perspective of historical impact, one should keep in mind the yawning gap between the reformist, almost social democratic tenor of Adorno the popular educator, and the pitch-black totality thinking of the philosopher Adorno. The one wrote about 'Heine the Wound' and on 'Was bedeutet: Aufarbeitung der Vergangenheit' ('What Does Coming to Terms with the Past Mean?'); the other worked in solitude and freedom on *Negative Dialectics* and the posthumously published *Aesthetic Theory*.

Analytic philosophy fared no better – though in a different way – in the early Federal Republic. It was weakly anchored at the institutional level, and ultimately prevailed in the centre of the discipline, not directly, but only by the roundabout route of a phenomenologically mediated appropriation of Frege's semantics. Besides essays by Günther Patzig, the work of Ernst Tugendhat was especially important in this regard. Nowadays, the analytical school with its standards dominates the argumentation of the entire discipline; to this extent, with the tailwind from the United States and Great Britain, it even emerged during the 1970s as the winner in the now overcome competition between the schools.

The situation in sociology was different from that in philosophy. After large numbers of its exponents had been driven out of the university departments, sociology first had to be rebuilt with the assistance of the returning émigrés: in Munich with the anthropologist Emerich K. Francis, a professing Catholic with a Jewish background, in Göttingen with Helmuth Plessner, in Cologne with René König, and in Frankfurt with Horkheimer and Adorno. In Münster and at the

Sozialforschungsstelle Dortmund, a productive scholar such as Helmut Schelsky, along with Hans Freyer and Arnold Gehlen, represented both in person and in substance a continuity within the discipline that had extended through the Nazi period. In this constellation, all concerned were aware of the contemporary historical background, so that the academic controversies also had political connotations from the beginning.

Unlike in philosophy, the Institute of Social Research, in which Horkheimer established a degree programme for sociologists, formed an equal pole in the tension-filled triangle 'Cologne–Münster–Frankfurt'. As I recall, the major controversies in the discipline during the first postwar decades were played out within this intellectual field of tension. Moreover, important for the decisive influence of Jewish émigrés was a controversy that followed on from a formally polite discussion between Adorno and Popper during the workshop of the German Sociological Association in 1961 in Tübingen; but if only because of these proponents, the so-called positivism controversy did not unfold along the aforementioned fronts rooted in political biographies.

Two Initial Sparks

In order to comprehend the scale of the public influence of Jewish émigrés, one must look beyond the walls of the university. However, in the diffuse medium of the public sphere, indicators that could provide orientation are much less distinct than *intra muros*. Therefore, I will mention just two events that seem to me in retrospect to have provided initial sparks for momentous advances in the political culture of the Federal Republic. I cannot deny the subjective element of my assessment in singling out two academic events; first, the lecture series that was held in 1956 in parallel at the universities of Frankfurt and Heidelberg to mark the 100th anniversary of the birth of Sigmund Freud; and, second, the presentation by Herbert Marcuse at the Deutscher Soziologentag in Heidelberg in the summer semester of 1964. In my estimation, the relevance of these two events goes beyond the merely biographical level of my personal impressions.

Max Horkheimer along with Alexander Mitscherlich had invited the international elite of psychoanalysis from the United States, England and Switzerland to present a lecture cycle. The brilliant lectures by René Spitz, Erik Erikson, Michael Balint, Ludwig Binswangen, Gustav Bally, Franz Alexander and others broke like an intellectual flash flood from a foreign world over the early Federal Republic. This is how it appeared at any rate from the perspective of a young man who had become acquainted with Freud only from a nebulous distance and as the name of a scientific street urchin. In order to understand the intellectual excitement of the audience, one must recall that at that time psychoanalysis was undergoing its scientific golden age and was internationally recognized as a key discipline for explaining anthropological and socio-psychological, and also in the broadest sense political, questions. Of course, intellectual impulses do not operate directly. But from then on analytical arguments forced their way into public discourses and constituted an important ferment within the arduous remembrance processes of a German society that was only learning to confront its still 'recent' past.

Incidentally, the series concluded with two lectures by a philosopher on 'The Idea of Progress in the Light of Psychoanalysis', which electrified me like scarcely any other lecture before or since. This was the first time that I saw Herbert Marcuse, who lectured on ideas from his still unpublished book *Eros and Civilization*. I had begun my work at the Institute just two months before. Now a vital contemporary spirit from its forgotten past confronted me, unexpectedly and without dialectical embellishment. The picture that we retain of Marcuse from the activist period of the student movement unjustly obscures the quality of the scholar who had received a solid philosophical training with Heidegger in Freiburg. Within the circle of 'old' members of the Frankfurt School, Marcuse was the one who adhered to conventional scientific standards in his philosophical studies. His book *Reason and Revolution* from the early 1940s – in a sense the parallel action to Löwith's *From Hegel to Nietzsche* – is the best example of this. Without this scientific quality, Marcuse's lecture on 'Industrialization and Capitalism' eight years later would not have met with the response among the younger generation that interests me in the present discussion of historical impacts.

At the sociology conference in Heidelberg in 1964, so it appears to some observers in retrospect, Max Weber had been, in a sense, installed as a classic. Be that as it may, this meeting of legendary figures in the discipline like Talcott Parsons, Raymond Aron and Herbert Marcuse, who delivered the keynote addresses, amidst the assembled German sociologists was at any rate an event of major intellectual importance. At its centre was, in turn, a controversy conducted essentially between Jewish émigrés – between Herbert Marcuse, on one side, and the astute Reinhard Bendix, backed up by Parsons and Benjamin Nelson, on the other. I recall that the year 1964 fell in the incubation period of the student movement. At that time, there was not yet any talk of 'capitalism'; the preferred term was 'advanced industrial society'. The first books by Adorno had appeared in the edition suhrkamp, but as yet none by Marcuse. The Socialist German Students' Union was not yet controlled by the actionists but instead by the most dedicated and most brilliant students in the discipline. I do not know how many of them were hearing 'their' Marcuse for the first time.

Marcuse stuck meticulously to Weberian texts in laying bare the secret paradigmatic core of old Critical Theory – a Weber-Marxism that promised to uncover the internal connection between formal rationality, domination and capitalism. At any rate, sitting in the audience, I sensed how this hermeneutic exercise caused a spark to leap across to the young minds, much as had happened to me during the Freud lectures. Regardless of how we now assess the ambivalent aspects of the public impact of Freud and of Marcuse's Marx and Max Weber, the two events mentioned were a condensation of the elusive and extremely indirect influence that, in rare moments, the intellectual translation of scientific work can have on public discourses.

Of course, careful empirical studies would be needed in order to test the concluding generalization that I can base solely on my own life experience. My impression is that the political culture of the old Federal Republic owes the hesitant progress it made in civilizing its attitudes in good, perhaps decisive, part to Jewish émigrés. It owes this happy outcome chiefly to those who were magnanimous enough to return to the country that had driven them out. One or two academically 'fatherless' generations learned from them how to distinguish the traditions that are worthy of being continued from a corrupt intellectual heritage.

9

Martin Buber – A Philosophy of Dialogue in its Historical Context[1]

On 24 November 1938, Martin Buber, who had emigrated to Israel in the nick of time, wrote to his friend Ludwig Strauss: 'To judge by a necessarily vague message from Frankfurt, our entire possessions in Heppenheim seem to have been destroyed'.[2] The November pogroms probably mark the deepest caesura in Buber's long and productive career. The further twenty-seven years of his life in Israel undoubtedly weigh heavily in the second part of this biography. But the sixty-year-old Martin Buber was already a world-renowned figure when he reached this safe harbour. At this point, he could already look back on a full life that had been devoted from the beginning to the Jewish cause in the German-speaking world. This circumstance may explain the honourable, but by no means self-evident, invitation to a German colleague to deliver the first lecture in this newly established series. For this, I would like to express my gratitude to the members of the Academy.

Historical accounts of Jewish culture in the German Empire and in the Weimar Republic depict Martin Buber not only as a leading figure in the Zionist movement but more specifically as the authoritative spokesman of a

Jewish cultural renaissance that was mainly supported by a younger generation.[3] The Young Jewish movement that took shape around 1900 within the orbit of the other youth and reform movements understood this awakening as the birth of a modern Jewish national culture. The twenty-three-year-old Buber made himself their spokesman when he held his first programmatic speech at the Fifth Zionist Congress in Basel in 1901. Since his publications on Rabbi Nachmann's Hasidic stories and the legend of Baalschem, he was also seen by a wider public as the spiritual leader of so-called cultural Zionism. In 1916 Buber realized the long-cherished plan to publish a Jewish monthly. *Der Jude* provided the intellectually ambitious platform that brought together such diverse writers as, for example, Franz Kafka, Arnold Zweig, Gustav Landauer and Eduard Bernstein.

His friendship with Franz Rosenzweig acquired major importance. The latter had returned from the war with his book *The Star of Redemption* and opened the Jüdisches Lehrhaus in Frankfurt in 1920, which was destined to become the model for similar institutions throughout the republic. With his programme of 'New Learning', Rosenzweig lent the impulses of the contemporary adult education movement a direction that could not fail to be congenial to Buber. As he proclaimed in his opening address, Rosenzweig supported 'a learning in reverse order. A learning that no longer starts from the Torah and leads into life, but the other way round: from life, from a world that knows nothing about the Law, or pretends to know nothing, back to the Torah. This is the sign of the time.'[4] Rosenzweig secured Buber as a permanent lecturer and as his closest collaborator. The famous Bible translation based on the characteristic features of the Hebrew language was also the fruit of their cooperation.

Viewed in retrospect, the list of lecturers at the Lehrhaus includes almost exclusively famous names – among others, Leo Baeck, Siegfried Kracauer, Leo

Strauss, Erich Fromm, Gershom Scholem, Samuel Josef Agnon, Ernst Simon and Leo Löwenthal. If we now read in Michael Brenner's historical study[5] that Martin Buber was at the time the 'most prominent teacher' amongst this circle and 'the most famous German-Jewish thinker of the Weimar period', we don't need to scratch our heads over a letter written by the dean of the philosophical faculty of the University of Frankfurt in support of Buber. When in 1930 Walter F. Otto applied to the ministry to transform the lectureship in the philosophy of religion that Buber had occupied since 1924 into a salaried honorary professorship, he could confine himself to the laconic statement that there was nobody more suitable than Buber, 'who is so well known that one can dispense with a detailed description of his achievements'.[6] Martin Buber resigned from this chair in 1933, immediately following the 'Machtergreifung', without awaiting the purge that would strip the University of Frankfurt of a third of its faculty.

A couple of years before I began my academic career at this same university as Adorno's assistant, I encountered Martin Buber on a single occasion (though of course only as one among a large audience of students). Buber had returned to Germany for the first time after the war and the Holocaust. Time and again, my wife and I have cast our minds back to this memorable evening in Lecture Theatre number 10 at the University of Bonn – less so to the content of the lecture than to the act of appearance, when the clamour in the overflowing auditorium abruptly fell silent. The entire auditorium rose to its feet in reverence when the President of Germany, Theodor Heuss, as if to underline the extraordinary nature of the visit, solemnly escorted the comparatively small figure of the white-haired and bearded old man, the sage from Israel, on the long passage past the row of windows to the podium. This was how we had imagined the Old Testament prophets as children. In memory, the entire evening contracts into this single dignified moment.

What I failed to understand at the time was that this scene also embodied an essential idea of Buber's philosophy, namely, the power of the performative, which overshadows the content of what is said. I must confess that my present-day reflections on the public role that Martin Buber played in the early Federal Republic are tinged with a certain ambivalence. In those years he featured centrally in the Jewish–Christian encounters, which as it happened were able to pick up where his earlier, similar initiatives from the Weimar era had left off. These encounters were certainly not devoid of serious substance and they will have prompted many people to engage in critical reflection. On the other hand, they fit into the then-pervasive intellectual climate which responded to a muddled need for an inward-looking and unpolitical assimilation of the 'recent past' – a genre to which Adorno, not without reason, attached the label 'jargon of authenticity'. In postwar Germany, Martin Buber, the reconciliatory religious interlocutor, was the antipode to the inexorable Gershom Scholem, who during the 1960s opened our eyes to the reverse side of the casual invocations of the so-called German-Jewish symbiosis.

Ladies and gentlemen, you have not invited me here to speak on the religious author and wise man, the Zionist and popular educator, Martin Buber. Martin Buber was a philosopher as well, and as such he was rightly admitted to the pantheon of the Library of Living Philosophers, the important series of books edited by Paul Arthur Schilpp that is held in high regard in the profession. Among those already honoured at the time were John Dewey, Alfred North Whitehead, Bertrand Russell, Ernst Cassirer, Karl Jaspers and Rudolf Carnap. Martin Buber was the twelfth laureate when he was admitted into this illustrious circle towards the end of his life, and some of the best minds in the discipline engaged in the discussion of his work.[7] At the centre of the discussion was, and still is, the I–You relation around which Buber's philosophical thought crystallized. I will begin by situating this idea in the history of philosophy (I). Then I would like to explain the systematic import of this founding idea by hinting at the implications that can be drawn from this approach quite independently of Buber's own interests (II). Finally, I will briefly characterize the philosophical achievements of religious authors as translators from one domain into the other. For, in Martin Buber's case, the humanist grounding of his Zionism can be understood in terms of the translation of particular religious intuitions in philosophical concepts with which we make generalizations that are independent of religious communities (III).

I. The Orientation to the Performative

Buber wrote his dissertation on Nicholas of Cusa and Jakob Böhme. Aside from his love of Hasidism, which had been a response to the emergence of the Frankist sects inspired by Sabbatai Zevi,[8] the question arises of whether at that time Buber already had some inkling of the astounding affinity between the imagery of Jakob Böhme and Jewish mysticism to which Gerschom Scholem would later draw attention with an anecdote about the visit of the Swabian Pietist F. C. Oetinger to the kabbalist Koppel Hecht in the Frankfurt ghetto.[9]

Martin Buber himself describes the breakthrough to the major philosophical insight that would shape the remainder of his work as a kind of conversion extending throughout the years of the First World War. Whereas up to that point he had interpreted his basic religious experience in mystical terms as withdrawal into a situation beyond the ordinary, after this turn he was more afraid of the loss of self in the unification with the all-encompassing divine spirit. The place of this at once absorbing and dissolving contact was now to be taken by the practice of fervent prayer, that is, by a relationship to God that was as it were normalized, though not levelled down. Contrary to speechless mystical experience, this relation of the person who prays to God as to a second person is mediated by words and 'the word', an idea that would be important for the remainder of Buber's philosophical thought.

In his old age Buber described his repudiation of mysticism in stark terms:

> Since then I have given up the 'religious' which is nothing but the exception, the extraction, exaltation or ecstasy . . . The mystery is no longer disclosed . . . it has made its dwelling here where everything happens as it happens. I know no fullness but each moral hour's fullness of claim and responsibility. Though far from being equal to it, I know that in the claim I am claimed and may respond in responsibility . . . If that is religion then it is simply all that is lived in its possibility of dialogue.[10]

These words summarize the inspiration underlying the reflections on which Buber had been working since 1917, and which he published in 1923 under the title *Ich und Du* (*I and Thou*). His later writings are footnotes to this major work. The interpersonal relation to God as the 'eternal You' structures the linguistic network of relations in which every person always already finds himself or herself as the interlocutor of other persons: '[T]o be man means to be the being that is over against.'[11]

As the use of personal pronouns shows, however, the situation of human beings in the world is conditioned by the fact that this 'being over against' must be differentiated into two different attitudes, depending on whether the 'interlocutor' in a particular case is other persons or other objects. The interpersonal relation between a first and a second person, between an 'I' and a 'You', is different in kind from the objectifying relation between a third person and an object, between an 'I' and an 'It'. For any interpersonal relation calls for the reciprocal interpenetration of the perspectives that those involved direct to each other, while each participant can adopt the perspective of the other. For it is part of the dialogical relation that the person addressed can assume the role of the speaker, just as, in turn, the speaker can assume that of the addressee. In contrast with this symmetry, the observer's gaze is fixed in an asymmetrical fashion on an object, which, after all, cannot return the gaze of the observer.

On the trail of this difference between the I–You and the I–It relation, Buber also discovers a corresponding difference between the roles of the respective subjects who say 'I'. In the one relation, the 'I' features as an actor; in the other, as an observer. An actor must 'enter into' an interpersonal relation and 'perform' this relation in a speech act. This performative aspect of the act of speaking is different from the content and the object of communication. We must distinguish the performative from the content aspect of the conversation. Because those involved do not spy or eavesdrop on each other like objects, but instead open themselves up for one another, they encounter each other on the social forum disclosed by dialogue and, as contemporaries, become narratively involved in each other's stories. They can both occupy the same place in social space and historical time only when they encounter each other as second persons in this performative attitude. Moreover, such an 'encounter' assumes the form of making the other present in his or her entirety. Thus, this making the other present as a person forms a horizon within which the perception of the other is first selectively focused on the features that are essential for the individual person herself, instead of shifting at will from one detail to another, as in the case of the observation of an object.

Buber describes this *priority of the performative in the encounter* in somewhat flowery terms: 'The primary word *I–Thou* can only be spoken with the whole being. The primary word *I–It* can never be spoken with the whole being.'[12] To be sure, the observer also acts insofar as he has to 'adopt' an objectifying attitude towards the object; but *in actu*, the performative aspect disappears for him completely behind the object itself, the theme of his perception or judgement. *Intentione recta* the observer disregards his own situation; by contemplating something in the world 'from nowhere' as it were, he abstracts from his own anchoring in social space and lived historical time. However, Buber recognizes that this first move of juxtaposing 'actor' and 'observer' is too simple. Even acting subjects often have an armour-plated ego and do not let their guard down. They, too, can screen themselves off and treat their interlocutor not as a second person but like an object from a third-person perspective – whether in an instrumental sense, like a doctor who operates on the body of a patient, or strategically, like a bank employee who foists a loan on an unsuspecting customer.

From the perspective of a cultural critic, Buber even fears that these monological modes of action could become the dominant mode of interaction in society as a whole. Against the overall sceptical attitude towards the progressive expansion of the social domains of strategic and purposive-rational action in the course of social modernization,[13] Buber's practical interest focused narrowly on a couple of outstanding face-to-face relationships, chiefly friendship or love. Even though such exemplary relations constitute only a marginal segment within the set of communicative actions, they interpret what Buber calls 'dialogical being'. The salient features of the ideal type of an unprotected encounter 'turned toward each other' in authentic togetherness are the performative aspects that are otherwise hidden by the thematic or content aspects of the conversation or interaction.

Buber shares this attention to the performative with other versions of contemporary existential philosophy, which equally try to uncover, under the 'what' of the supposed 'essence' of human beings, the buried mode and modality of this life, the 'how' of its being-in-the-world. This oscillates in turn between authentic and inauthentic being. For what sets human life apart is that it must be led and that it can fail. Phenomenology, historicism and pragmatism have a common interest in the performative character of life as it is lived. In this respect, all of these philosophers remain heirs of the Young Hegelians, who began the movement of de-transcendentalizing and deflating reason – what Marx called the 'decomposition' of Hegel's absolute. This whole philosophical movement situates reason itself in social space and historical time. It focuses on how reason is embodied in the human organism and social practice, that is, on how communicatively socialized subjects cooperatively deal with the contingencies and conflicts in their environment. Buber was as alert to this Young Hegelian heritage as to the affinity with contemporary existential philosophy. He engaged with Feuerbach, Marx and Kierkegaard as intensively as with Jaspers, Heidegger and Sartre. What sets him apart within this extended family, however, is the attention he paid to the communicative constitution of human existence, which he describes, following Wilhelm von Humboldt and Ludwig Feuerbach, in terms of a philosophy of dialogue.[14]

II. The Implicit Idea:
The Primacy of the Second Person

The point of departure is the phenomenon of being spoken to: 'Life means being addressed'[15] in such a way that the one must 'confront' the other, and this in a two-fold sense. The person addressed must allow himself to be confronted by the other by opening himself up to an I–You relation in the first place; and then he must take a stance on what this other says to him – in the most straightforward case by answering 'yes' or 'no'. In the willingness to be *called to account* by another person and to be answerable to her, the person addressed exposes himself to the non-objectifiable presence of the other and recognizes her as a non-representable source of autonomous claims. At the same time, he submits himself to the semantic and discursive commitments imposed by language and dialogue. In the process, the reciprocity of the reversal of roles between addressee and speaker lends the dialogical relation an egalitarian character. The willingness to accept the dialogical obligations imposed by the other, therefore, is bound up with a pattern of attitudes that is as egalitarian as it is individualist. However, Buber is not painting an irenic picture. Specifically in intimate relations, the other must be taken seriously in her individuated nature and be recognized in her radical otherness.[16] In the need to balance the two contradictory expectations – 'the spreading of one's own stubborn uniqueness and turning back to connection'[17] – Buber identifies the source of the unease lurking in every kind of communicative socialization.

To be sure, the religious author radicalizes the philosophy of dialogue into the 'true conversation' in which the finger of God is at work; but the inquiry of the philosopher also offers interesting points of contact for the deflated postmetaphysical mode of analysis. In the intervening years, the relevant discourses have branched out in different directions. Let me begin with the highly controversial question: what is more fundamental, self-consciousness and the epistemic relation of the self to itself or, as Buber claims, the communicative relation to the other in dialogue? Which of the two can claim priority over the other – monological self-relation or dialogical mutuality? In his 1964 postdoctoral dissertation, Michael Theunissen positioned Buber's philosophy of dialogue as an alternative approach to Husserl's derivation of the lifeworld from the constitutive acts of the transcendental subject.[18] It is not just in order to meet a local interest that I can discuss the systematic point of contention also with the help of the question that Nathan Rotenstreich once posed to Martin Buber – namely, '[W]hether reflection itself is but an extraction from the primacy of mutuality or whether mutuality presupposes reflection.'[19]

In classic mentalist terms, Rotenstreich defends the primacy of self-consciousness against the interpersonal relation. According to the mentalist argument, realizing a relation between a first and a second person presupposes that the subject who is capable of using 'I' has already made the differentiation between himself and another subject; and this act of differentiation presupposes in turn an antecedent epistemic relation to self, because a subject cannot distance himself from other subjects without first having perceived and identified himself as a subject.[20] As the fraught tenor of Buber's detailed response to his Jerusalem colleague reveals, this controversy is not a matter of one question among others but turns on a deep-seated paradigm dispute. Are human beings basically cognitive subjects who first relate to themselves reflexively in the same objectifying attitude as they relate to something in the objective world? In that case, their primary distinguishing feature from other living beings is self-consciousness. Or does one subject first become aware of himself as a subject in communication with the other? In that case, it is not self-consciousness but language and the corresponding form of communicative socialization that set our species apart from its closest relatives, and hence constitute the distinguishing feature of human existence as such.

Martin Buber does not conceive of human beings primarily as subjects of cognition but as practical beings who have to enter into interpersonal relations in order to cope, through cooperation, with the challenges of the contingencies of the objective world. Human beings are distinguished also in his view by the ability to take a distance from themselves, but not in the form of self-objectification: 'It is incorrect to see in the fact of primal distance a reflecting position of a spectator.'[21] What sets human beings apart from animals is not self-reflection in the sense of turning a reiterated subject–object or I–It relation back upon oneself. Our lives are instead performed in the triadic communicative relation between a first and a second person who are communicating with one another about objects in the world.[22] The phenomenon of self-consciousness is derived from dialogue: 'The person becomes conscious of himself as sharing in being, as co-existing.'[23] In advance of any explicit self-reflection, the subject is caught up in interpersonal dialogical relations and first becomes aware of himself performatively by adopting the perspective of the other towards himself: 'The I that [first] emerges is aware of itself, but without reflecting on itself so as to become an object.'[24]

Buber has a rather special justification for the priority of the dialogical relationship over self-consciousness – namely, the a priori of prayer. Buber accords the relationship to the 'eternal Thou' a constitutive status. And because the encounter with the original word of God structures all possible conversations within the world, Buber can assert: 'Nothing helps me so much to understand man and his existence as does speech'[25] – note 'speech' and not language as such! Like Franz Rosenzweig, Buber participates in his own way in the linguistic turn in twentieth-century philosophy. Understandably enough, he has no interest in a semantics that, in Richard Rorty's words, is merely the continuation of seventeenth-century epistemology with language-analytical means. Wittgenstein's turn to the use of language was more congenial to Buber's view.[26] Buber had the important and correct intuition that, without the dialogically created 'between' of an intersubjectively shared background, we cannot achieve objectivity of experience or judgement – and conversely.

With his analysis of the twofold perspective of the I–You/I–It relation, Buber draws attention to the constitutive interpenetration of two equally fundamental relations: what is constitutive for the human mind is the interpenetration of the intersubjective relation between addressee and speaker, on one side, with the respective intentional and objectivating relation to something in the world about which they communicate, on the other. The mutual perspective taking between I and You makes possible the sharing of intentions towards objects in the world, while the individual perceptions of something in the world acquire their objectivity only by virtue of the fact that they are shared between different subjects. This complex relationship is reflected in the competent use of the system of personal pronouns and of the associated (temporal and spatial) referential terms. Competent speakers' knowledge of how to use personal pronouns and deictic expressions, which provides the pragmatic frame for any possible communication, depends on the systematic interpenetration of the I–You and I–It relations.

Allow me to mention in passing an empirical confirmation of this philosophical proposition, which is very close to Buber's fundamental insight. In psychological experiments on language development,

Michael Tomasello has demonstrated the relevance of a triadic relation for interactions with children at the pre-linguistic stage. This relation is produced through the symbolic linkage of the vertical relation to the world (I–It) with the horizontal relation to the other (I–You) between the participants in communication, on the one hand, and their respective relations to the object of communication, on the other.[27] Children of around twelve months follow the pointing gesture of caregivers (or themselves use their index finger) to draw the attention of the other person to certain things and to share their perceptions with him or her. At the horizontal level, mother and child also grasp each other's intentions through the direction of gaze, so that an I–You relation – that is, a social perspective – arises which enables them to direct their attention to *the same* object in the vertical I–It direction. By means of the pointing gesture, soon also in combination with mimicry, children acquire knowledge that is shared intersubjectively with the mother of the jointly identified and perceived object, from which the gesture then ultimately acquires its conventional meaning.

III. The Philosophical Work of the Religious Author

Martin Buber did not pursue the obvious path of developing his dialogical-philosophical approach in terms of a philosophy of language further.[28] Nathan Rotenstreich had already criticized him, not entirely without justification, for focusing on the performative aspect of the I–You relationship, on the 'how' of the 'making-present' of the other person, and neglecting the cognitive aspect of the I–It relation, that is, the representation of states of affairs and the corresponding truth claims. The well-founded critique of the fixation of the major philosophical tradition on the cognitive grasp of beings, the self-reflection of the knowing subject and the representative function of language often slides too quickly in Martin Buber into cultural criticism. He throws the baby out with the bathwater when he lumps together all *objectifying* stances on the world with the *objectivistic* trends of the age and exposes them to blanket suspicion. On the other hand, there is a trivial reason why Buber did not exhaust the theoretical potential of his own approach, namely, his overriding interest in issues of an ethical-existential self-understanding. The weak normativity which, already as such, is inherent in the pragmatics of linguistic communication is eclipsed by the strong ethical normativity of binding oughts and authentic life projects.

Buber the philosopher is inseparable from the religious author. Buber belongs to the small set of distinguished religious authors with philosophical ambitions, extending from Kierkegaard, Josiah Royce and William James, through the young Ernst Bloch, Walter Benjamin and Emmanuel Levinas, up to contemporaries such as Jacques Derrida. These thinkers continue under the changed conditions of modernity a labour of translation that could be conducted in an inconspicuous, osmotic fashion as long as, after the closure of the Academy, Greek metaphysics was administered and developed under the auspices of the theologians of the Abrahamic religions. Once this fragile symbiosis was dissolved by nominalism, the subversive and regenerative force of an assimilation of religious semantics to the rational discourse of philosophy could unfold only in the broad daylight of advancing secularization.

The philosophers now had to 'out' themselves as religious authors, as it were, if they wanted to save untapped semantic contents from the well-articulated wealth of the great axial religions by translating them into generally accessible philosophical concepts and discourses. Conversely, a pluralistic public can learn something from these authors only because they pass religious intuitions through a philosophical sieve as it were and thereby strip them of the specificity and exclusivity lent them by their original religious communities. This *modern role of the religious author as translator* may also explain the position that Martin Buber assumed in the political public arena. His controversy with Herzl is well known. For Buber, the Zionist project was more than just a political undertaking aimed in the first place at founding a state and later at the self-assertion of a sovereign Jewish state. Not every interpretation of cultural Zionism was incompatible with such a project; on some readings, cultural Zionism was only meant to complement national power politics. But the incompatibility Buber saw was justified from the perspective of a religious author who wanted to ground the project of a Jewish national culture in the concepts of a philosopher. He was interested in a justification of Zionism not only from an ethno-national, 'inward-looking' perspective, but one couched in normative terms and with arguments intended to convince everybody.

For Buber, the Zionist idea had to be justified in humanist terms. That would be unsurprising from a Kantian point of view. But Buber was no more a Kantian or a neo-Kantian than Gershom Scholem, Ernst Simon or Hugo Bergmann. These German-Jewish intellectuals saw themselves as Jewish Jews who took their inspiration, in the spirit of a contemporary philosophy of life, from Herder's early romantic discovery of nation, language and culture, rather than directly from the tradition of the Enlightenment or from Marx and Freud. From their perspective, the meagre rational substance that Kant, Cohen and science had left of their religion was too little. For them, the mystical underside of religion or the dark side uncovered by Bachofen was more interesting. On the other hand, they had forgotten neither the household deities that presided over their parental homes – Spinoza and Lessing, Mendelssohn and Kant, Goethe and Heine – nor the nationalist motives for the everyday discrimination to which they had been exposed in their European homelands. The moral sensitivity with which this first generation of cultural Zionists reflected on the so-called Arab problem from the outset, and discussed and analyzed it passionately to the end of their lives, testifies to a rather cosmopolitan and individualist perspective from which they wished their national project to be understood.[29]

Admittedly, Buber, the existential philosopher, did not have an adequate sociological conceptual frame at his disposal. He treats 'the social', too, against the backdrop of an ideal-type embodying – as the counterpart to the authentic I–You relationship – an 'essential We'.[30] Yet outlines of a political theory are discernible. In 1936, while still in Germany, Buber subjected Carl Schmitt's friend–foe idea to a devastating critique. He recognized that these categories appear 'at times when the political community is threatened', but 'not at times when it is assured of its survival'. Therefore, the friend–foe relation is not fit to serve as the 'principle of the political', according to Buber. This resides instead 'in the striving (of a political community) toward the order proper to it'. But the communal life founded in language and culture still has priority over Hegel's *Not- und Verstandesstaat*, the institutions of the modern state: 'The person belongs to the community into which he was born or in which he lands, whether he wants to make something of this or not.'[31]

Nor is there any necessary, much less a normatively justified, correlation for Martin Buber between a nation that evolved or coalesced and a state that is consciously constituted by its citizens. It is well known that Buber at one point was very much open to the idea of a binational state for Israel.[32] Regardless of whether it be a nation or state, the normative justification of all social and political forms of coexistence is ultimately measured for him by the authentic and considered positions of the individual members. What is right or wrong in the political as well as the moral sense is founded in the 'interpersonal space' of dialogue. Each individual must conscientiously bear a responsibility the group cannot relieve him of. This individualism finds expression in the remarkable statement that true belonging to the community 'includes the experience of the limits of this belonging', an experience, however, 'that escapes definitive formulation'.[33]

This humanist vision could not be easily reconciled with the political realities; and after the foundation of the state, the goal of a single state that would unite citizens of Jewish and Arab nationality on an equal footing had lost its foundation. On this initial reading, the political humanism of those German-Jewish outsiders who had been influential within the educational system is a closed chapter. Does this also hold for the philosophical stimulus that informed this high-minded programme? To be sure, something of Martin Buber's spirit still lives on in the weak discourse of academia under different assumptions and in a different theoretical context (I am thinking, for example, of Chaim Gans's book on the 'morality of the Jewish state').[34] We must acknowledge without sentimentality that traditions come to an end; only in exceptional situations can they be recovered with a 'tiger's leap into the past', and then of course only in a new interpretation and with different practical consequences. With the image of a tiger's leap, Walter Benjamin was thinking of the seizing hold 'of a memory such as it flashes up at a moment of danger'.[35] Perhaps this beautiful and endangered country, which is overflowing with history, has simply too many memories.

10

Our Contemporary Heine

'There are No Longer Nations in Europe'[1]

(1) In 1828, Heine noted on his journey to Genoa: 'day by day the ridiculous national prejudices are disappearing; all harsh peculiarities are perishing in the universality of European civilization. There are no longer nations in Europe but parties, and it is wonderful to behold how these ... recognise each other, and make themselves mutually intelligible, notwithstanding the difference of language' (II.376).[2] These words were written 184 years ago. In the meantime we have even entered a new millennium – sufficient time for a mutual understanding to have developed among European peoples, one should think. But Heine's optimism seems ridiculously exuberant when confronted with the abject spectacle of burgeoning national egoisms during the current banking, financial and sovereign debt crisis. Where else if not in the European Parliament, which exists in the meantime but has been pushed to the sidelines by the heads of government, should the far-sighted statement that there are no longer any nations, only parties, have acquired institutional force? Only here, not in the European Council that has monopolized all power, could generalized social interests develop across national borders and thwart the 'ridiculous national prejudices'.

Of course, Heine was always careful to distinguish 'national prejudices' from 'patriotism' or 'love of one's country'. Thus he defended, albeit with reservations, the Hambach Festival, where 'French liberalism delivered its most intoxicated Sermons on the Mount' (IV.88), while noting that 'Teutomania prevailed' at the meeting at the Wartburg, where chauvinistic German students staged a book burning.[3] Later, he conceded: 'Out of hatred of the champions of Nationalism I could almost love the Communists' (V.233).[4] Heine admired French patriotism and envied the fact that the French could paint the love of their homeland in cosmopolitan colours because they were able to idealize their native country as the cradle of civilization and human progress. Conditions in Germany appeared all the more grim to the émigré Heine.

On the other hand, the pain of emigration turned Heine into a herald of the German genius. He, who contributed to restoring Romanticism to the Enlightenment as its true property through his own work, extols the German character. Even though he captivates the reader through the splendour of his fluid style and is not at a loss for moving, suggestively lilting, mellifluous words, he specifically lauds, in contrast to the French, the severity, combativeness and inner turmoil of such distinctive German spirits as Luther and Jakob Böhme, Jean Paul and Fichte, Kleist and Grabbe. The culmination of German intellectual history is for him, of course, the Age of Enlightenment, of which he boldly asserts that 'nowhere, not even in Greece, was the human intellect permitted to develop itself and to express its thought as freely as in Germany from the middle of the last century till the French invasion' (III.542).[5]

This affirmative attitude towards the best among German traditions is for me the key to the happy constellation that, after the Second World War, finally led to an unbiased Heine reception also in Germany. It was only after 1945 that Heine, who was revered in France and in the rest of the European countries, and even on other continents, during his lifetime, could find full recognition among us Germans. To be sure, Heine's fanfare for Europe, summoning the troops to storm the barricades of nationalist prejudices, has fallen on deaf ears until now. But regardless of this special form of deafness, for which Heine as it happens had already coined the term 'disenchantment with Europe', the narrow-minded defensiveness against Heine the intellectual first began to crumble in the defeated and morally depleted postwar Germany. The younger generations had a sympathetic ear for authors who were able to guide them through the ruins of the discredited and mistrusted traditions to the uncorrupted parts of their battered national heritage. This time, too, the best traditions had been cultivated by Jewish émigrés in exile. And those who returned had Heine in their luggage. The series extends, to mention just a couple of the intellectuals, from Adorno and Günther Anders, through Marcel Reich-Ranicki, to Peter Szondi and Ivan Nagel in my generation.

Heine was the author who in 1828 provided a succinct answer to the question: 'What is the great question of the age?': 'It is that of emancipation. Not simply the emancipation of the Irish, Greeks, Frankfurt Jews, West Indian Negroes ... but the emancipation of the whole world, and especially that of Europe, which has attained its majority' (II.376).[6] Who could have been a better guide for young Germans after the end of fascism than someone whose favourite author was Lessing? In 1835, Heine, who had met Hegel and Schelling in person, published in Paris a wonderful panorama, *On the History of Religion and Philosophy in Germany*, painted in broad brush strokes. Like a good family doctor, in this work he sounded out the vital organs of recent German intellectual history. And, in order to ensure that his French readers did not lose their foothold while negotiating this precarious ridge, in the manner of a prudent mountaineer he stretched a safety rope leading past the German precipices and secured it at one end with Spinoza and at the other with Hegel.

Between these two fixed points, the trails of the struggle for religious freedom, for freedom of thought and the press, and for human rights, lead unfalteringly from Spinoza via Christian Wolff in the first instance to Lessing, the 'prophet who pointed the way from the New or Second Testament to the third'. What Heine says about Lessing could just as well have applied to himself: 'Lessing was the living criticism of his time, and his whole life was a polemic' (III.585).[7] This is followed by the enthusiastic vindication of the bookseller Christoph Friedrich Nicolai, whose valiant fight against obscurantism sometimes also led him to fight against windmills; and Heine leads us further, via the great Jewish enlightener Moses Mendelssohn and the freedom-loving Georg Foster, to the destroyer of worlds, Immanuel Kant. Although according to the Hegel student Heine Kant was no genius, in the 'heavy, buckram style' of his *Critique of Pure Reason* he stormed the heavens and put its entire crew to the sword. This Robespierreian revolution in the world of the mind then found its continuation in Fichte, the Napoleon of philosophy, and Schelling, the counter-revolutionary, and culminated in the contemporary, 'Orléanian', regime of Hegel. However, since Kant prompted this great intellectual movement less by the content of his writings than performatively, as it were, 'by the critical spirit that pervaded them',[8] now, after the death of Hegel and the July Revolution in France, a whole generation of young Germans and Young Hegelians committed to the present was poised at the threshold separating the thoughts of the revolution from the performance of the revolutionary act.

With this curriculum, Heine had developed a counter-programme to the mainstream of the whole nineteenth century and the early twentieth century out of the sources of German and – considering the enormous impact of Spinoza among the educated Jewish middle class – German-Jewish intellectual history. After 1945, this programme contrasted even more sharply with everything that had led to the German catastrophe, and with much of what led a servile, but tenacious, afterlife – disguised as repressive anti-communism – among the remnants of the Nazi elites who survived into the Adenauer era. Never was the 'party of flowers and nightingales' that Heine charged with revolutionary sentiment more attractive, never was the emphatic unity of democracy, human rights, cosmopolitan hope and pacifism more convincing, never was social emancipation, the 'great soup question', more self-evident than for those who were searching for the intellectual roots of these ideas in the shadow of the crushed Nazi regime.

This is not to suggest that the Heine reception in the old Federal Republic of Germany went smoothly. Even as late as the 100th anniversary of the poet's death, the German government covered its back with an ambivalent press release. Still, a short time later, in 1956, the meritorious Heinrich-Heine-Institut was founded in Düsseldorf. Moreover, a critical edition of Heine's works edited by Klaus Briegleb Heine appeared in West Germany. But without the resonance that Heine's song of praise to the 'democracy of terrestrial gods, equal in glory, in blessedness, and in sanctity'[9] found among the libertarian spirits of the 1968 movement, it is unlikely that Heine's work *as a whole* would have enjoyed an enduring rehabilitation. Historians speak today of a consolidation of the Heine renaissance in the 1970s and of a canonization in the 1980s. In Gerhard Höhn's *Heine-Handbuch*, the pioneering achievement by a private scholar, one can read that, by the end of the 1980s, the 'controversy over Heine' had long since turned into its opposite: 'The champion of freedom and progress is no longer maligned today, but is instead everywhere celebrated and honoured.'[10]

These words were delivered on the 190th anniversary of Heine's birth. What has this canonized Heine, honourably buried under mountains of interpretations, to say to us on his 215th birthday? To be sure, with his *New Poems*, the *Romancero*, the *Harz Journey* and *Germany: A Winter Tale*, the poet Heine is quite capable of looking after his own literary reception. But Heine was not only a poet. Can he still provide guidance in the role of a tribune who shapes mentalities? Does the secular apostle, does the biography of his work steeped in the history of his time, have anything left to say to us? Do we still have something to learn in this sense from Heine, or at least from the example he set?

(2) This is not a rhetorical question. It has never been easy to say something about Heine which he had not already said about himself long before. Heine was both mercilessly self-critical and self-indulgent. He reflected tirelessly about himself, his role, his person and his work; and, despite the pitfalls of narcissistic self-absorption, what he said about himself was seldom completely off the mark.[11] Hence, every interpreter runs the risk of following paths already paved in the autobiographical writings. This dilemma is in itself remarkable, because it is explained by the fact that Heine was the first major author *to express a new consciousness of time*. Heine was one of the first poets to give expression to a new time consciousness in the age of the emerging mass media. The historical consciousness that made its debut with the French Revolution became the determining force of his writing. This consciousness of living in a new, indeed the 'newest', time (as Hegel put it) is reflected in the modernization of literary genres, hence in Heine's letters, 'travel pictures', salon reports and confessions, on the one hand, and it infuses the familiar poetical forms with partisanship, turning them

into 'time poems' [*Zeitgedichte*], on the other. The nervous consciousness of a topicality oriented towards progress and the future, uncoupled from the past, gives rise to the well-known tension in Heine's work, mistakenly criticized by Karl Kraus, between journalism and poetry.

Heine was an intervening author caught up in the struggles of his time. He saw contemporary history as 'hunting history' [*Jagdgeschichte*]: 'Now it is time to hunt down the liberal ideas on a grand scale' (II.667). With an eye to his audience, Heine reflected on his role in the maelstrom of current events continually made present by journalism. He knew that he was writing in the resonance chamber constituted by a well-informed, partisan reading public.[12] And he polarized his readers because he wrote his works in the expectation of provoking dissonant reactions. This reflexivity, the reflection in the eyes of opinionated readers, also predestined Heine for the role of a perspicuous autobiographer whose observations about himself are always one step ahead of us posthumous interpreters. But what really sets Heine apart is the combination of the polemical mindset of a political writer with the pathos of truth of a sensitive poet who makes himself into the incorruptible seismograph of his own emotions. The empathetic lyrical 'I' who finds voice in Heine's songs and in many of his later poems plays the foil to the partisan contemporary, even where it becomes the sounding board of contemporary history. The lyrical 'I' wants to be a mere witness and to express what emerges from the depths of one's subjectivity as a recurring experience which is shared by many, and hence is universal.

The new time consciousness to which Heine gives literary voice makes him into our contemporary. With him we share the modern consciousness of a dynamic flow of time that, like Benjamin's angel, rushes towards present generations from the future, tearing them out of the past and confronting them with the demand to choose responsibly between alternatives and find the right answer within the horizon of their respective futures. At the same time, contemporaries understand the engine that accelerates the flow of time in this way as 'modernity'. They want to take control of this process, whether in order to slow down modernization or to speed it up. From this perspective, contemporary history acquires not only the character of an appeal that the present must confront. The process of history simultaneously acquires a direction, with some peoples belonging to the vanguard, while others are left behind. There is now a benchmark against which progress is measured, and the simultaneity of the non-simultaneous is measured against the most progressive. It is a well-known fact that, for Heine, German philosophy was nothing but the dream of the French Revolution. And Marx would observe that the Germany of this time was 'below the level of history' and belonged in the 'junkroom of modern nations'.[13]

The dimensions of the past and the future acquire negative or positive values for contemporaries depending on what weights they attach to the gains and losses they expect from modernization. This political colouring of the dimensions of time first found a spatial representation in the seating arrangement of the French National Assembly. The conservatives separated themselves from the liberals. The one side was convinced that the losses entailed by the disintegration of traditional ways of life outweigh the gains promised by a chimerical progress. The others objected that the average net gains of creative destruction far outweighed the suffering of the losers of modernization. Finally, what set the Left apart was its sensitivity to the paradoxes of progress: the wounds inevitably inflicted by social modernization could be healed only by the revolutionary leap into true modernity.

This was also Heine's view. The uprooted ways of life of the past contain an inviolable substance that the men of action can rescue for future generations only if they are guided by a dialectical interpretation of progress. Heine's mentality is profoundly marked by this ambivalence between longing for the overdue overthrow of the repressive forces of the nobility and the Church, which at this time were stifling progress, and the desire to rescue a vulnerable, because non-renewable, human heritage that must remain beyond the reach of fanatical iconoclasts. Heine, who was enchanted by the July Revolution, certainly celebrates the break with the past: 'All reverence for tradition will be renounced' (III.590). However, when he arrived in Paris after the revolution, he first made his way to the Bibliothèque Royale, where he requested to see the 'Manessische Handschrift' and the manuscripts of the troubadours.

We remain contemporaries of this modern time consciousness. Nothing has changed in the political colour theory and the seating arrangement in parliaments, which continue to reflect the profit-and-loss calculation of an economically trivialized progress. To be sure, in view of the global alignment of social infrastructures, it is tempting to say that today all societies are modern. But failed development aid programmes, and especially the failure of naïve and over-hasty attempts to export democratic institutions and procedures indiscriminately all over the world, have taught us about the non-simultaneity of cultural traditions and mentalities. However reluctant we are to make value judgements about other cultures, we nevertheless continue to apply the standard of modernization as a matter of course, at least in the economic measures of unit-labour costs and competitiveness. Every day we read about the 'backwardness' of the Southern European countries compared to the exporting countries of the North.

There has also been little change in the soup kitchens

for the poor, now more discreetly called 'food banks'. However, the revolutionary pathos that was still in the first flush of youth in Heine's time has been used up. Behind Heine was the French Revolution that had matured into the Napoleonic Code; behind us are the mountains of corpses of the oppressed and the murdered piled up during the Age of Extremes. We are living in a post-revolutionary and a post-heroic age. By 1968, the revolution had already changed genres – from opera to operetta. What changed in the process was not time consciousness as such, but consciousness of modernity, that is, the attitude of political actors to the time arrow of economic and social modernization. Since then, modernization has assumed the form of a self-sustaining systemic process. And we are no longer supposed to be able to take control of it. The locus of control has shifted from courageous intervention to despondent accommodation. We no longer relate to our future in the mode of challenge and response, but – as the German Chancellor maintains – in the mode of TINA: *there is no alternative.*

At this point, however, Heine specialists might warn against cheap polemics and turn the tables: wasn't it Heine who, in his 'mattress grave', revoked his youthful revolutionary fantasies of creating the kingdom of heaven on earth? Didn't he recognize the error of inflating claims and making excessive demands on our political forces? Didn't he expiate the sin of self-deification with his late conversion to belief in a personal God? In view of the limits of political intervention and organization, wouldn't a good measure of fatalism, or at any rate self-restraint, have even spared our peoples the extremes of the twentieth century?

These questions suggest not only a false picture of Heine, but also the wrong conclusions. Instead of political claims extending into the realms of phantasy, we are now confronted with a politics in avoidance mode. We are all cowering under the demands of the financial markets and, by keeping still, are confirming the seeming impotence of a mode of politics that makes the bulk of the taxpayers pay for the damage of the financial crisis instead of the speculators. Heine would have poured scorn over the bookkeepers of privatized profits and socialized costs. What would he, who also *appreciated* the backward glance of Romanticism, have said about the decision of the proud city of Stralsund to sell off its medieval treasures to private collectors because its public coffers are empty? And what would he have said about the poor East London borough of Tower Hamlets, which is hawking a sculpture endowed by Henry Moore for the same reason? The neo-conservative warning against normative excesses is not the correct response to a normatively disarmed *Zeitgeist* that has been converted to the imperatives of the market and self-exploitation. But above all, in Heine's late turn to religion I discern something quite different from accommodating submission to higher powers. We need to take a closer look at the *Confessions* in order to establish what the late Heine actually revoked – and what he remained true to.

(3) Heine dated his religious turn to the year 1848 – when the revolution failed and his debilitating illness simultaneously entered an oppressive phase. Until then, Heine had hoped for a radical upheaval. Although the people had fought for the triumph of the bourgeoisie in July 1830, it had not benefited from this victory. Viewed from this almost Marxist perspective, the revolution that brought Napoleon III to power was a failure. Heine ruefully observed: 'A revolution is a misfortune, but a still greater misfortune is a failed revolution' (IV.78). Quite apart from his personal motives, Heine's disappointment with the 1848 revolution was not without historical justification, at least when it came to his native country. It would be another century before a

democracy could gain a permanent foothold on German soil.

Heine's political differences with the 'German Jacobins' in Paris at the time also became aggravated against this pessimistic background. In his treatise against Börne, Heine had ridiculed the ugly ash-grey hospital habit they had adopted as a uniform. In this pamphlet he had warned against a 'radical cure that, in the end, only works externally'.[14] The fear of the fury of violent egalitarianism and anti-artistic iconoclasm that had only simmered until 1848 ('they will fell my laurel groves and plant potatoes in their place', V.232)[15] began to boil, so to speak, after the – in Heine's view failed – revolution of 1848. It became one of the motives that would lead him 'in those days of general madness' to revise his convictions concerning a *philosophy of the deed*.

Until then, Heine had assimilated Hegel's philosophy of mind as the delineation of a process of human beings' self-deification. On this reading, Hegel is supposed to have taught 'how man becomes God through cognition, or, what amounts to the same thing, how God in man attains to self-consciousness' (VI.I.479 and II.510).[16] Heine, who was impressed by Saint-Simonism, was convinced that he was merely divulging the 'secret doctrine' of German idealism when he – as one of the first Young Hegelians – proclaimed the imperative to proceed from thought to action, from theory to practice. However, this philosophical idea of a radical upheaval had a Romantic tinge in Heine's lyrical 'I' from the beginning. The party of flowers and nightingales was supposed to ensure the reconciliation of social justice with beauty and happiness. The dream of reconciling Jerusalem and Athens that Hegel, Hölderlin and Schelling had shared in the seminary in Tübingen was finally supposed to be fulfilled. 'Spiritualism' was finally supposed to become fused with 'sensationalism', as Heine now put it, hence the egalitarian liberation of society with the emancipation of the senses and the flesh. This utopia continued to resound later in the desire to reconcile 'Jewish asceticism' with 'Hellenic naturalism'. But Heine would now renounce the extravagant revolutionary idea of hybrid self-deification. Now he could give free rein to the fear of revolution that he had suppressed until then. Thus, in 1854, Heine admitted that: 'Like many other dethroned gods of that period of upheaval [i.e., the years 1830–48], I had sorrowfully to abdicate, and to retire once more into private life as a human . . . I returned to the humble folds of God's creatures, and I paid homage to the power of a great Almighty Being' (VI.I.475).[17]

Of course, the bedridden Heine also reflected on the infirmity of the invalid in need of help as a much less convincing motivation for his repentance. Formerly he had scoffed that 'So many freethinkers . . . have been converted on their deathbed' (III.634),[18] and now he had crawled on his knees to the cross himself. Thus, the touching, almost childlike lament that he intones in his mattress grave cannot completely efface the malicious doubt awakened in him by the charitable intent of his religious conversion. The melody of Heine's confession is, like everything else, self-deprecating:

> In this state, it is a true blessing for me that there is someone in heaven in whose ears I can complain, especially after midnight, when Mathilde has sought the rest she so badly needs. Thank God that I am not alone in such hours, and I can pray and whine without hindrance and shame. (VI.I.476)[19]

This tenor also pervades the Lazarus Heine's treatment of his condition *post-mortem*. We owe one of his most beautiful poems to this soothing, almost reconciled melancholy (VI.I.113):

Not a mass will be sung for me
Not a *Kaddish* will be said,

None will say or sing a service
On the day that I lie dead.

But on some such day it may be,
If good weather is foreseen,
Ma'am Mathilde will go strolling
On Montmartre with Pauline.

She will come to deck my grave with
Immortelles, and say with sighs:
'*Pauvre homme!*' and wipe a tear drop
Of damp sorrow from her eyes.

But, alas, I shall be living
Too high up – there'll be no seat
I can offer to my darling
As she sways on weary feet.

Oh you sweet and chubby child, you
Must not walk home all the way;
You'll see coaches standing ready
At the barrier gate that day.[20]

(4) This would be a beautiful and fitting end to a lecture on Heine, but there is still one loose end to be tied up. Although Heine renounced an extravagant idea of revolution, he remained faithful to his fight, the fight for the political enforcement of human rights, the 'Ten Commandments of the new world faith'. He remained true, as he put it himself, to 'the same democratic principles to which I was devoted in my earliest youth'.[21] When Heine in his old age laments the weaknesses of the sovereign people, he continually interrupts himself and in passing develops the entire social democratic programme of the time to come. He already sounds just like Brecht: 'that ugliness [of the people] simply comes from dirt, and will disappear as soon as we open public baths, in which His Majesty, the people, may gratuitously bathe himself' (VI.I.468).[22] Whatever significance

the religious turn may have had for Heine personally, intellectually speaking, replacing Homer with the Bible meant that he gave his unabated political radicalism a deeper normative anchoring. Now Heine took seriously Kant's insight that the 'living law of morality and the source of all law and all authority' must be stripped of its merely subjective character. A different kind of objectivity is proper to morality and law than that of art derived from subjectivity.

Heine had always toyed with a religious attitude. He had attributed the role of 'apostles' of a religion of freedom to intellectuals and writers from the outset. In his old age he realized that, in doing so, he had assimilated essential impulses from the Old Testament, in good atheistic manner, with the help of Saint-Simon and Hegel. In the 'morality of ancient Judaism' he now recognized the egalitarian and universalist roots of his own militant pathos of justice and freedom. Heine the convert did not have to make any major revisions to his view of history, even though he now no longer resisted Protestant conversion and Jewish descent, and both even appeared in an affirmative light: the Jews bestowed their God and his word, the Bible, as a gift on the world. Later, in the course of the Reformation, the book of books was translated into all languages – and was distributed across the globe and entrusted to 'the exegesis of individual reason'. In the end this promoted 'that grand democracy wherein each man shall not only be king in his own house, but also bishop' (VI.I.485).[23]

Above all, however, Moses now assumed a larger-than-life presence for Heine. Liberty had always been 'the great emancipator's leading thought' and this idea, Heine wrote, 'breathes and glows in all his statutes concerning pauperism'.[24] Of course, Heine cannot desist from his old game of playful teasing even in the face of death. Every reader of his poems has the experience that Heine initially entices her into succumbing to the

ingratiating and desublimating allure of his moving
tone, but that at the latest in the closing line he breaks
the enchanting spell to prevent the reader, who is on
the point of succumbing, from drifting into sentimentality. Heine, because he still feels the itch of Feuerbach's
criticism of religion, even throws such a tongue-in-cheek
'last line' into his homage to Moses: 'May God forgive
the sacrilegious thought, but sometimes it appears to me
as if this Mosaic God were only the reflected radiance
of Moses himself, whom he so strongly resembles in
wrath and in love' (VI.I.480).[25] However we understand
Heine's religious turn, one thing it is not: it is not a defla-
tion of the claim to an improvement of this world. At the
end of his life, Heine postponed the longing of the poet
for happiness, which had always been religiously tinged,
to the hereafter. But that did not mark a break with the
balladeer's enthusiasm for liberty, or with the political
ire and the militant revolt of the intellectual and citizen
whose sense of justice has been injured. He made no
concessions when it came to his Kantian-inspired philosophy of history with a cosmopolitan intent. Nothing
suggests that he felt less distain in his old age than in
younger years for the disconsolate realism of those who
'shake their heads over our struggles for freedom', or
that he had relented in the fight against the fatalism of
those for whom there is 'nothing new under the sun'.
His polemic against the conception of history 'of the
worldly-wise men of the historical school', the Savignys
and Rankes, remains in force: 'They mock all the efforts
of a political enthusiasm that wants to make the world
better and happier' (III.21).

   In his darkest moments, the ageing Heine may have
thought that not even the existing shabby balance
between good and evil could be maintained if we do not
try our utmost to make the world better in spite of everything without being afraid of making fools of ourselves.
'Improving the world' has always had a pejorative ring

in Germany. Today, at a time of frenzied stagnation, this concept has an especially strident overtone. Under the weight of the crippling complexity of a 'God become money' (Heine), the mood of resignation is spreading that nothing works any more even though everything is changing. Every thought that looks beyond the present is suspect. Yet, a century after Heine's abortive revolution of 1848, we saw that progress was possible, at least in the domain of legality. Heine's anticipatory liberal notions of democracy in Germany have prevailed. Why shouldn't his European notions of overcoming national prejudices with the aid of the cunning of economic reason be able to come true?

When Heine travelled to Poland as a twenty-five-year-old student at the invitation of a friend, he was deeply moved by the exuberant patriotism he encountered there. In view of the unhappy fate of this nation divided for the third time, he exclaimed: 'These death throes of the body of the Polish people are a terrible sight!' However, compassion did not prevent him from observing at the same time:

> [A]ll the peoples of Europe and of the whole world will have to survive this death struggle if life is to spring from death, and if Christian fraternity is to spring from pagan nationality. I do not mean renouncing all beautiful particularities that are the best reflections of love [of one's country], but that ... universal brotherhood of man, original Christianity, to which our most noble tribunes, Lessing, Herder, Schiller, etc., have given the best expression. (II.80f.)

This is what we can still learn from Heine today.

Notes and References

Preface to the English Edition

1 Jürgen Habermas, *The Crisis of the European Union – A Response* (Cambridge: Polity, 2012); Habermas, *Europe – The Faltering Project* (Cambridge: Polity, 2009).
2 Claus Offe, *Europe Entrapped* (Cambridge: Polity, 2014).
3 Available online at: <http://www.coe.int/t/dgal/dit/ilcd/archives/selection/churchill/ZurichSpeech_en.asp>.

Chapter 1 The Lure of Technocracy: A Plea for European Solidarity

1 Justine Lacroix and Kalypso Nicolaides (eds), *European Stories: Intellectual Debates on Europe in National Contexts* (Oxford: Oxford University Press, 2010).
2 I have been defending this alternative for over two decades. See, for example, Jürgen Habermas, 'Citizenship and National Identity' (1990), in *Between Facts and Norms*, trans. William Rehg (Cambridge, MA: MIT Press, 1992), 491–515,

here 500–7; 'The Postnational Constellation and the Future of Democracy', in *The Postnational Constellation*, trans. Max Pensky (Cambridge: Polity, 2001), 58–112; *The Crisis of the European Union: A Response*, trans. Ciaran Cronin (Cambridge: Polity, 2012).

3 European Commission, 'A Blueprint for a Deep and Genuine Economic and Monetary Union: Launching a European Debate', COM (2012) 777 final / 2; available online at: <http://ec.europa.eu/commission_2010-2014/president/news/archives/ 2012/11/pdf/blueprint_en.pdf>. Cited in the following as 'Blueprint'. This confusing paper shows signs of having been hastily cobbled together.

4 This state of affairs is expressed elegantly in the 'Blueprint' (2): 'EMU is unique among modern monetary unions in that it combines a centralized monetary policy with decentralized responsibility for most economic policies.'

5 This was already noted at an early stage by Henrik Enderlein, *Nationale Wirtschaftspolitik in der europäischen Währungsunion* (Frankfurt am Main: Campus, 2004).

6 To this corresponds the authority of the Commission 'to require a revision of national budgets in line with European commitments' ('Blueprint', 26); this competence is clearly intended to go beyond the already existing obligations to exercise budgetary discipline.

7 'Blueprint', 35.

8 The 'Let me have my cake and eat it too' strategy adopted by the proposal of the Commission shirks the overdue decision ('Blueprint', 13): 'Its deepening should be done within the Treaties, so as to avoid any fragmentation of the legal framework, which would weaken the Union and question the paramount importance of EU law for the dynamics of integration.'

9 The 'Convergence and Competitiveness Instrument' ties the targeted financial support to contractual arrangements between the individual member states and the Commission ('Blueprint', 21ff. and Annex 1).

10 'Blueprint', 27ff. and Annex 3.

11 An emblematic expression of the pseudo-autonomy of the member states and of how the increase in power of a free-floating executive answerable only to the European Council undermines democratic legitimation is the proposal for a 'Convergence and Competitiveness Instrument' (CCI) that Angela Merkel also embraced at the World Economic Forum in Davos (January 2013). According to this proposal, the necessary country-specific support based on 'the dialogue between Commission and Member States' ('Blueprint', 21) would be made contingent in each case on a contractual arrangement between the Commission, on the one side, and the individual applicant state, on the other.

12 See the relevant works of Wolfgang Streeck, most recently: 'On Fred Block, "Varieties of What? Should We still be Using the Concept of Capitalism?"', in Julian Go (ed.), *Political Power and Social Theory* 23 (2012): 311–21; *Buying Time: The Delayed Crisis of Democratic Capitalism*, trans. Patrick Camiller (London: Verso, 2014).

13 Wolfgang Streeck, 'Von der Demokratie zur Marktgesellschaft', *Blätter für deutsche und internationale Politik* 12 (2012): 61–72.

14 Stefan Oeter, 'Föderalismus und Demokratie', in Armin von Bogdandy and Jürgen Bast (eds), *Europäisches Verfassungsrecht* (Heidelberg: Springer, 2009), 73–120.

15 See my essay 'The Crisis of the European Union in Light of a Constitutionalization of International Law – An Essay on the Constitution for Europe',

in Jürgen Habermas, *The Crisis of the European Union*, 1–70, especially 28–44.

16 Christoph Möllers, *Die drei Gewalten: Legitimation der Gewaltengliederung in Verfassungsstaat, Europäischer Union und Internationalisierung* (Wielerswist: Velbrück, 2008), 158ff.

17 The procedural argument is still the least dishonourable reason for the inability of the European Council to master the crisis in a cooperative manner. The only reason why the political failure of the Eurozone governments has yet to assume historical proportions is a barely legitimate intervention by the ECB.

18 For an interesting analysis, though one still coloured by a national historical perspective, see Andreas Rödder, 'Dilemma und Strategie', *Frankfurter Allgemeine Zeitung*, 14 January 2013, 7.

19 Claus Offe, 'Europa in the Trap', trans. Samuel Willcocks, *Eurozine*, 2 February 2013, available online at: <http://www.eurozine.com/articles/2013-02-06-offe-en.html>.

20 Konstantinos Simitis, 'Flucht nach vorn', in *Frankfurter Allgemeine Zeitung* (27 December 2012), available online at: <http://m.faz.net/aktuell/politik/die-gegenwart/eurokrise-flucht-nach-vorn-12007360.html>.

21 In the constitutional state, legal norms are of course also supposed to satisfy the further condition of legitimacy, so that they can be followed not only out of motives of legality, but also from 'respect for the law' – with a view to the democratic procedure of generating the norms.

22 Andreas Wildt, 'Solidarität – Begriffsgeschichte und Definition', in Kurt Bayertz (ed.), *Solidarität: Begriff und Problem* (Frankfurt am Main: Suhrkamp 1998), 202–17, here 210ff.

23 In earlier publications, I connected moral justice too closely with solidarity/ethical life. See Habermas,

'Justice and Solidarity: On the Discussion Concerning Stage 6' (1984), in Thomas E. Wren (ed.), *The Moral Domain: Essays in the Ongoing Discussion between Philosophy and the Social Sciences* (Cambridge, MA: MIT Press, 1990), 224–50. I no longer support the assertion that 'Justice conceived deontologically requires solidarity as its reverse side' (244) because it leads to a moralization and depoliticization of the concept of solidarity. On this, see also my commentary on Maria Herrera Lima in Habermas, 'Religion und nachmetaphysisches Denken: Eine Replik', in *Nachmetaphysisches Denken II: Aufsätze und Repliken* (Berlin: Suhrkamp, 2012), 127ff., here 131–3.

24 Habermas, 'On the Relation between the Nation, the Rule of Law, and Democracy', in *The Inclusion of the Other: Studies in Political Theory*, trans. Ciaran Cronin (Cambridge, MA: MIT Press, 1998), 129–53.

25 Hauke Brunkhorst speaks of the 'transformation of solidarity in the medium of law' (*Solidarität unter Fremden* [Frankfurt am Main: Fischer, 1997], 60ff.).

26 This background of social rights in solidarity reappears when social achievements are revoked. The chairman of the Charité Hospital in Berlin, Karl Max Einhäupl, rightly employs the concept of solidarity when, in an interview published in the *Frankfurter Allegmeine Zeitung* on 30 December 2012, he places in question the equal treatment of patients – hence their rights – in connection with the rising costs of medical technology: 'We will have to renounce solidarity to a certain extent. But as a society we have to consider how we can limit the damage to solidarity as much as possible. The decision over who gets what must not be left up to individual doctors' (Christiane Hoffmann and Markus

Wehner, '"Bislang kann jeder Patient alles haben", Interview mit Charité-Chef Karl Max Einhäupl', in *Frankfurter Allgemeine Sonntagszeitung* [30 December 2012], 2). Why does he not speak in terms of justice here? Clearly, already today it is left up to the moral sense of justice of individual doctors whether they provide their publicly insured patients with the same treatment and with equally effective drugs as their privately insured patients who have the same condition. Legal sanctions still apply when unequal treatments – as in the extreme cases of the organ donor scandals in Germany – have fatal consequences for the disadvantaged patients. In the interview, the clinic head deliberately speaks in terms of solidarity rather than of law and morality. When it comes to his theme – that is, the delicate, not to say egregious, issue of selecting patients for an expensive treatment from among all of those suitable for treatment – he would like to shift the responsibility from individual doctors to the political system. Hence he adopts the collective perspective of the citizen body as a whole instead of that of the individual. What brings the issue of solidarity into play is the reference to *the entire patient body*, all of whose members – were it ever to reach the stage that some of them could enjoy life-saving privileges at the expense of others – are citizens of the same political community.

27 I have in mind the concept of political justice developed by John Rawls.

28 See the entries in the subject index of Klaus Briegleb's edition of the works of Heinrich Heine (*Heinrich Heine: Sämtliche Schriften,* Vol. VI [Munich: Hanser 1976], II, 818).

29 Hauke Brunkhorst, *Solidarity: From Civic Friendship to Global Legal Community*, trans. Jeffrey Flynn (Cambridge, MA: MIT Press, 2005).

30 Karl H. Metz, 'Solidarität und Geschichte: Institutionen und sozialer Begriff der Solidarität in Westeuropa im 19. Jahrhundert', in Bayertz (ed.), *Solidarität*, 172–94; for an in part critical treatment, see Wildt, ibid., 202ff.

Chapter 2   European Citizens and European Peoples: The Problem of Transnationalizing Democracy

1 For an account of this deficiency that focuses on the legal branch of the international governance network, see Armin Bogdandy and Ingo Venzke, *In wessen Namen? Internationale Gerichte in Zeiten des globalen Regierens* (Berlin: Suhrkamp, 2014). For a general treatment, see Jürgen Habermas, 'Keywords on a Discourse Theory of Law and of the Democratic Constitutional State', this volume, ch. 3, 46–60, here 55ff.

2 Wolfgang Streeck *Buying Time: The Delayed Crisis of Democratic Capitalism*, trans. Patrick Camiller (London: Verso, 2014).

3 The startling decisions taken by the first G20 summit in London in November 2008 under the impact of the banking crisis that had just broken out have predictably remained without consequences. International agreements between states are insufficient unless the coordination of divergent interests is also subjected to institutional regulation. Politics can take an effective stand against the imperatives of markets, which play the interests of different states off against one another, only by establishing institutions that generalize interests – that is, only by constructing supranational capacities for joint action.

4 Henrick Enderlein, *Nationale Wirtschaftspolitik in der europäischen Währungsunion* (Frankfurt am Main: Campus, 2014); Fritz W. Scharpf,

'Monetary Union, Fiscal Crisis and the Preemption of Democracy', *Zeitschrift für Staats- und Europawissenschaften* 2 (2011): 163–98; Scharpf, 'The Costs of Non-Disintegration: The Case of the European Monetary Union', in Annegret Eppler and Henrik Scheller (eds), *Zur Konzeptionalisierung europäischer Desintegration: Zug- und Gegenkräfte im europäischen Integrationsprozess* (Baden-Baden: Nomos, 2013), 165–84; Scharpf, 'Die Finanzkrise als Krise der ökonomischen und rechtlichen Überintegration', in Claudio Franzius, Franz C. Mayer and Jürgen Neyer (eds), *Grenzen der europäischen Integration* (Baden-Baden: Nomos, 2014), 51–60.

5 Eppler and Scheller (eds), *Zur Konzeptionalisierung Europäischer Desintegration*.

6 Recently on the 'shared sovereignty' line of argument, see Francis Chevenal, 'The case for Democracy in the European Union', *Journal of Common Market Studies* 51 (2013): 334–50. For critical accounts, see Daniel Gaus, 'Demoi-kratie ohne Demoskratie – welche Polity braucht eine demokratische EU?', in Oliver Flügel-Martinsen, Daniel Gaus, Tanja Hitzel-Cassagnes and Franziska Martinsen (eds), *Deliberative Kritik – Kritik der Deliberation: Festschrift für Rainer Schmalz-Bruns* (Wiesbaden: VS-Verlag, 2014), 297–322.

7 Jürgen Habermas, *Between Facts and Norms*, trans. William Rehg (Cambridge: Polity, 1996).

8 Ingeborg Maus, *Zur Aufklärung der Demokratietheorie* (Frankfurt am Main: Suhrkamp, 1992); Maus, *Volkssouveränität: Elemente einer Demokratietheorie* (Frankfurt am Main: Suhrkamp, 2011).

9 The Federalist Papers are often used as a reference point in discussions of European law: see Christoph Schönberger, 'Die Europäische Union als Bund',

Archiv des öffentlichen Rechts 129 (2004): 81–120; Schönberger, 'The European Union's Democratic Deficit between Federal and State Prohibition', *Der Staat* 48 (2009); Robert Schütze, 'On "Federal" Ground: The European Union as an (Inter)National Phenomenon', *Common Market Law Review* 46 (2009): 1069–105.

10 However, the centuries-old ambivalence over whether 'We the people of the United States' (in the preamble to the US Constitution) must not be interpreted in the sense of the totality of the 'peoples' of the individual states suggests that, empirically speaking, the alternative between the citizens of the American nation taking precedence over the citizens of the states and, conversely, the state peoples taking precedence over the heterogeneous nation of an immigrant society, remains open.

11 Interestingly enough, migration research is currently discovering that citizenship status is the crucial dimension of social integration for immigrants. This status is the point of reference for the communication strategies of official naturalization policy. Daniel Naujolis, *Migration, Citizenship, and Development* (New Delhi: Oxford University Press, 2013), shows this, using the integration of people from India into the United States as an example.

12 Habermas, 'Public Spheres beyond the Nation-State?', in *Europe – The Faltering Project*, trans. Ciaran Cronin (Cambridge: Polity, 2009), 181–3.

13 Drawing on Ulrich K. Preuss ('Europa als politische Gemeinschaft', in Gunnar Folke Schuppert, Ingolf Pernice and Ulrich Haltern (eds), *Europawissenschaft* [Baden-Baden: Nomos, 2005], 459ff.), Claudio Franzius ('Europäisches Vertrauen? Eine Skizze,' *Humboldt Forum Recht*, Aufsätze 12 (2010): 159–76) develops the concept of a 'transaction-we in the sense of a we of others' for supranational federations.

14 I introduced the idea of a form of popular sovereignty split at the root in Jürgen Habermas, *The Crisis of the European Union: A Response*, trans. Ciaran Cronin (Cambridge: Polity, 2012), 28–53.

Chapter 3 Keywords on a Discourse Theory of Law and of the Democratic Constitutional State

1 This is the revised introduction to a seminar devoted to *Between Facts and Norms*, which took place from 11 to 14 February 2013 at the Max Planck Institute for Comparative Public Law and International Law in Heidelberg.

2 See James Bohman and William Rehg (eds), *Deliberative Democracy: Essays on Reason and Politics* (Cambridge, MA: MIT Press, 1997); see for additional literature the following excellent essay: Stefan Rummens, 'Staging deliberation: The role of representative institutions in the deliberative democratic process', in *The Journal of Political Philosophy* 20/1 (March 2012): 23–44.

3 Claus Offe, 'Participatory Inequality in the Austerity State: A Supply-side Approach', in Armin Schäfer and Wolfgang Streeck (eds), *Politics in the Age of Austerity* (Cambridge: Polity, 2013), 196–218.

4 See the reflections I develop in 'The Crisis of the European Union in Light of a Constitutionalization of International Law – An Essay on the Constitution for Europe', in Habermas, *The Crisis of the European Union: A Response*, trans. Ciaran Cronin (Cambridge: Polity, 2012), 1–70.

5 On this division of the development of international law, see Anne Peters, *Völkerrecht* (Zürich: Schultheiss, 2006), 11ff.

6 Legal pluralist approaches have traced these changes back to displacements in relations of power between

the public authority of the state and the private economic power of globally operating companies, and, as public–private partnerships have increased, have made the over-hasty diagnosis that the legislative authority of the state is becoming diffused. The disenchanting effect of the banking crisis was not the first phenomenon to prompt a reassessment in discussions in international law of the role of 'public authority' in international relations. See Armin von Bogdandy, Philipp Dann and Matthias Goldmann, 'Developing the Publicness of Public International Law: Towards a legal framework for global governance activities', in *German Law Journal* 9/11 (2008): 1375–1400; on the 'public turn' in general, see Nico Krisch, 'Global governance as public authority: An introduction', in *International Journal of Constitutional Law* 10/4 (October 2012): 976–87.

7　Immanuel Kant, 'Introduction to the Doctrine of Right', in Kant, *The Metaphysics of Morals*, ed. and trans. Mary Gregor (Cambridge: Cambridge University Press, 1996), 25 (Ak. 6:232).

8　See, with regard to international jurisdiction, Armin von Bogdandy and Ingo Venzke, 'Zur Herrschaft internationaler Gerichte: Eine Untersuchung internationaler öffentlicher Gewalt und ihrer demokratischen Rechtfertigung', in *Zeitschrift für ausländisches öffentliches Recht und Völkerrecht* 70 (2010): 1–49.

9　Christina Lafont, 'Alternative Visions of a New Global Order: What Should Cosmopolitans Hope For?', in *Ethics & Global Politics* 1/1–2 (2008): 41–60.

10　Peter Niesen (ed.), *Transnationale Gerechtigkeit und Demokratie* (Frankfurt am Main: Campus, 2012).

11　See my reflections on this in 'The Crisis of the

European Union in Light of a Constitutionalization of International Law'.

Chapter 4 The Next Step – An Interview

1 Interview with Claus Reitan and Hubert Christian Ehalt for *Die Furche* (Vienna) in May 2012.
2 Jürgen Habermas, *The Past as Future*, trans. Max Pensky (Lincoln, NE: University of Nebraska Press, 1994).
3 English translation: *The Postnational Constellation*, trans. Max Pensky (Cambridge: Polity, 2001).
4 Habermas, *Zur Verfassung Europas: Ein Essay* (Berlin: Suhrkamp, 2011); English translation: *The Crisis of the European Union: A Response*, trans. Ciaran Cronin (Cambridge: Polity, 2012).

Chapter 5 The Dilemma Facing the Political Parties

1 Speech delivered on accepting the Georg August Zinn Prize on 5 September 2012, in Wiesbaden, Germany.
2 Claus Hulverscheidt, 'Das Italienische an Herrn Monti', *Süddeutsche Zeitung* (30 August 2012), 4.
3 Quoted from Cerstin Gammelin, 'Wir durchbrechen den Teufelskreis', interview with EU Commissioner Michel Barnier, in *Süddeutsche Zeitung* (31 August 2012), 2.
4 Mario Draghi, 'So bleibt der Euro stabil! Die Europäische Zentralbank kann der Währung durch die Krise helfen', *Die Zeit* (30 August 2012), 1.

Chapter 6 Three Reasons for 'More Europe'

1 Contribution to the discussion of the 'Forum Europa' of the Association of German Jurists held on 21 September 2012 in Munich.

2 Herman Van Rompuy, 'Towards a genuine economic and monetary union: Report by President of the European Council Herman Van Rompuy', EUCO 120/12 (26 June 2012), available online at: <http://ec.europa.eu/economy_finance/crisis/docu ments/131201_en.pdf>.

3 I fail to understand why the Court bases its reasoning in the so-called Lisbon judgment on Article 38 (1) of the Basic Law (GG), which has nothing to do with the perpetuity clause. The latter only protects the participation of the federal states in the legislative process and the *principles of a constitutional state* laid down in Articles 1 and 20 of the Basic Law. The point at issue, therefore, is a normative substance that the Basic Law wants to preserve, but without specifying that this must be implemented within a national territory and in the form of a nation-state. The same normative substance could also be preserved within the framework of a supranational multilevel democracy, insofar as the member states retained the power to monitor it through their national constitutional courts. When taken in conjunction with Article 23 (1) GG, which calls upon the Federal Republic to cooperate in realizing a united Europe, Article 79 (3) GG cannot be plausibly read as a barrier to integration. Article 79 (3) GG refers to the principle of democracy *as such* formulated in Article 20 (2) GG, not specifically to the right to vote in elections to the German parliament. There is not a single word in Basic Law about a 'core identity' of the Federal Republic of Germany. There are good reasons why the concept

of sovereignty does not crop up in this context. The Lisbon judgment, by contrast, uses the concept of sovereignty as classically understood at various points. But hasn't the postwar development with Article 23 (1) GG rendered this reading obsolete? As international law is becoming constitutionalized, the traditional meaning of state sovereignty in international law is undergoing a transformation. Nowadays sovereignty should be understood as a reflection of popular sovereignty.

Chapter 7 Democracy or Capitalism? On the Abject Spectacle of a Capitalistic World Society Fragmented along National Lines

1 Wolfgang Streeck, *Buying Time: The Delayed Crisis of Democratic Capitalism*, trans. Patrick Camiller (London: Verso, 2014). The page numbers in the text refer to this edition.
2 Its characteristic features were full employment, sectoral wage agreements, employee co-determination, state control over key industries, a broad-based public sector with secure employment, an income and taxation policy that prevented glaring social inequalities, and, finally, public business cycle and industrial policy designed to prevent risks to growth.
3 On this, see Jürgen Habermas, 'Rettet die Würde der Demokratie', *Frankfurter Allgemeine Zeitung* (4 November 2011), available online under: <http://www.faz.net/aktuell/feuilleton/euro-krise-rettet-die-wuerde-der-demokratie-11517735.html>, 31.
4 Quoted from UK government, 'EU Reform: PM Takes Case to Madrid, Paris and Berlin' (8 April 2013), available online under: <https://www.gov.uk/government/news/eu-reform-pm-takes-case-to-madrid-paris-and-berlin>.

5 That is, 'Alternative für Deutschland' or 'Alternative for Germany' (trans.).

6 As a European citizen who followed the Greek, Spanish and Portuguese protests (at a comfortable distance) in the newspaper, however, I can share Streeck's empathy with the 'outbursts of rage' in the street: 'If democratically organized populations can behave responsibly only by giving up use of their national sovereignty, and by limiting themselves for generations to keeping their creditors happy, then it might seem more responsible to try behaving irresponsibly' (160).

7 In the meantime, however, the privatization of public services has advanced so far that this systemic conflict can be mapped less and less clearly on to the interests of different social groups. The sets 'people composed of national citizens' and 'people composed of market players' no longer coincide. The conflict of interest is increasingly leading to conflicts within one and the same person.

8 In 2005, at the height of the boom in speculative financial instruments, Josef Ackermann, then head of Deutsche Bank, declared that the bank had set itself the target of an annual return on equity capital of 25 per cent. This was widely criticized in Germany at the time as excessive and, especially in the light of the subsequent global financial crisis, as symptomatic of a reckless mindset in the financial sector (translator's note).

9 In what follows, I set to one side the economic consequences of winding up the euro. On this, see Elmar Altvater, 'Der politische Euro: Eine Gemeinschaftswährung ohne Gemeinschaft hat keine Zukunft', *Blätter für deutsche und internationale Politik* 5 (2013): 71–9.

10 Among the German 'tribes', the 'sedentary' Bavarians are said to be the oldest. However, DNA analysis

of bone findings from the late Migration Period, when the Bavarians were identified for the first time as such in historical records, have confirmed the so-called 'motley-crowd' [*Sauhaufen*] theory, 'which postulates that a late Roman core population coalesced with droves of migrants from Central Asia, Eastern Europe and Northern Germany to form a Bavarian tribe'. See Rudolf Neumaier, 'Mia san mia – aber woher? Das Volk, das plötzlich da war: Eine Archäologin gräbt die Multikulti-Wurzeln der Bajuwaren aus', *Süddeutsche Zeitung* (8 April 2013), 12.

11 The growing pluralism of forms of life, which provides confirmation of the increase in economic and cultural differentiation, contradicts the expectation that lifestyles are destined to become homogenized. The process by which corporatist forms of regulation are replaced by deregulated markets as described by Streeck has led to a boost in individualization that has attracted the interest of sociologists. Incidentally, this boost also explains the peculiar change in sides by 1968 renegades who succumbed to the illusion that they could live out their libertarian urges under conditions of market liberal self-exploitation.

12 The details may be in need of further consideration, but in spite of the misgivings of the German Federal Constitutional Court the general tendency is correct.

13 I developed this idea of a constitution-building sovereignty that is divided 'at the origin' – that is, already in the constitution-building process itself – between citizens and states, in 'The Crisis of the European Union in Light of a Constitutionalization of International Law – An Essay on the Constitution for Europe', in Habermas, *The Crisis of the European Union: A Response*, trans. Ciaran Cronin (Cambridge: Polity, 2012), 1–70; see also the essay 'Keywords on a Discourse Theory of Law and of

the Democratic Constitutional State' in the present
volume.

14 Among the 'cheap' alternatives is, for example, the
– in itself, not at all incorrect – recommendation to
introduce Eurobonds, currently being rehashed by
George Soros. This is being rejected in turn with the
correct argument, popular in Northern European
countries, 'that Eurobonds have a legitimation problem in the current political system; for that would
mean spending taxpayer money without consult-
ing the voters'. See Andrea Rexer, 'Die Schuld
für die Schulden. George Soros zur Euro-Krise',
Süddeutsche Zeitung (11 April 2013), available online under: <http://www.sueddeutsche.de/
wirtschaft/george-soros-zur-euro-krise-die-schuld-
fuer-die-schulden-1.1645930>, 1. This stalemate
blocks the alternative of creating the foundations
of legitimation for a change in policy that would
include Eurobonds.

Chapter 8 Jewish Philosophers and Sociologists as Returnees in the Early Federal Republic of Germany: A Recollection

1 Paper presented at a conference on 'Jewish Voices in
the German Sixties', organized by the Department
for Jewish History and Culture of the Ludwig-
Maximilians-Üniversität in Munich in June 2011.
2 In her novel *Landgericht* [*State Justice*] (Vienna:
Jung und Jung, 2012), Ursula Krechel has presented
an impressive account of the fate of one Jewish
returnee, an obscure district court director.
3 Publisher and, from 1959 onwards, director of
Suhrkamp Verlag (translator's note).
4 Elias, *Über den Prozeß der Zivilisation* (Frankfurt
am Main: Suhrkamp, 1976).

5 Strauss, *Gesammelte Schriften*, ed. Heinrich Meier (Stuttgart: Metzler, 1996–).

Chapter 9 Martin Buber – A Philosophy of Dialogue in its Historical Context

1 Talk delivered on the occasion of the first 'Martin Buber' Lecture at the Israel Academy of Sciences and Humanities on 1 May 2012 in Jerusalem.

2 Tuvia Rübner and Dafna Mach (eds), *Briefwechsel Martin Buber – Ludwig Strauß* (Frankfurt am Main: Luchterhand, 1990), 229.

3 Martin Brenner, *Jüdische Kultur in der Weimarer Republik* (Munich: C.H. Beck, 2000), 32ff.

4 Rosenzweig, 'Upon Opening the Jüdisches Lehrhaus', in *On Jewish Learning*, ed. Nahum Norbert Glatzer (Madison, WI: University of Wisconsin Press, 1955), 98.

5 Martin Brenner, *Jüdische Kultur in der Weimarer Republik*, 90, 96.

6 Notker Hammerstein, *Die Geschichte der Wolfgang Goethe-Universität Frankfurt am Main*, Vol. I (Neuwied: Luchterhand, 1989), 120.

7 Paul Arthur Schilpp and Maurice Friedman (eds), *The Philosophy of Martin Buber* (La Salle, Ill.: Open Court, 1967). Among the participants were Gabriel Marcel, Charles Harthorne, Emmanuel Levinas, Emil Brunner, Max Brod, Hand Urs von Balthasar, Jacob Taubes, C.F. von Weizsäcker, Helmut Kuhn and Walter Kaufmann.

8 On Martin Buber's interest in Hasidism, see Hans-Joachim Werner, *Martin Buber* (Frankfurt am Main, New York: Campus, 1994), 146ff.

9 Gershom Scholem, *Major Trends in Jewish Mysticism* (New York: Schocken, 1995), 238.

10 Buber, 'Autobiographical Fragments', in Schilpp

and Friedman, *The Philosophy of Martin Buber*, 26.

11 Ibid., 35.

12 Buber, *I and Thou* (New York: Continuum, 1957), 11.

13 'But in times of sickness it comes about that the world of *IT* is no longer penetrated and fructified by the inflowing world of *Thou* as by living streams but separated and stagnant, a gigantic ghost of the fens, overpowers man.' Buber, *I and Thou*, 56.

14 On Humboldt, see Buber, *Zwiesprache*, in Buber, *Das dialogische Prinzip*, 178; on Feuerbach, Buber, *Das Problem des Menschen* (Gütersloh: Gütersloher Verlagshaus, 1982), 58ff. On the stimuli that Buber received from his contemporaries, see especially Michael Theunissen, *The Other: Studies in the Social Ontology of Husserl, Heidegger, Sartre, and Buber*, trans. Christopher Macann (Cambridge, MA: MIT Press, 1984), §46.

15 M. Buber, *Zwiesprache*, 153.

16 Martin Buber, *Die Frage an den Einzelnen*, in Buber, *Das dialogische Prinzip*, 233f.; on this, see Werner, *Martin Buber*, 48ff.

17 *I and Thou*, 87 (my translation).

18 Theunissen, *The Other*, 266ff.

19 Nathan Rotenstreich, 'The Right and the Limitations of Martin Buber's Dialogical Thought', in Schilpp and Friedman, *The Philosophy of Martin Buber*, 124f.

20 Rotenstreich, 'The Right and the Limitations of Martin Buber's Dialogical Thought', 125f.: 'If we do not grant the status of consciousness of one's own self we are facing the riddle how could a human being realize that it is he as a human being who maintains relations to things and to living beings and is not just submerged but amounts to a twofold attitude of detachment (i.e., in the I–It-relation) and

attachment (in the I–Thou-relation) . . . How is it possible to be both detached and attached without the consciousness of oneself as a constitutive feature of the whole situation?'

21 Martin Buber, 'Replies to my Critics', in Schilpp and Friedman, *The Philosophy of Martin Buber*, 695.

22 Karl-Otto Apel, 'Die Logos-Auszeichnung der menschlichen Sprache: Die philosophische Tragweite der Sprechakttheorie', in *Paradigmen der Ersten Philosophie: Zur reflexiven – transzendentalpragmatischen – Rekonstruktion der Philosophiegeschichte* (Berlin: Suhrkamp, 2011), 92–137.

23 Buber, *I and Thou*, 52.

24 Buber, 'Replies to my Critics', in Schilpp and Friedman, 695.

25 Ibid., 696.

26 On this, see Part I of Apel, *Paradigmen der Ersten Philosophie*.

27 M. Tomasello, *The Cultural Origins of Human Cognition* (Cambridge, MA: Harvard University Press, 2000); Tomasello, *Origins of Human Communication* (Cambridge, MA: MIT Press, 2008).

28 Jürgen Habermas, *Philosophische Texte: Studienausgabe in fünf Bänden* (Frankfurt am Main: Suhrkamp, 2009), Vol. 2, *Rationalitäts- und Sprachtheorie*.

29 Buber, *Die Frage des Einzelnen*, 254f.

30 Buber, *Das Problem des Menschen*, 116.

31 Ibid., 241.

32 Steven Aschheim describes the position of the intellectuals united in Brit Schalom and later in Ichud (in *Beyond the Border: The German-Jewish Legacy* [Princeton, NJ: Princeton University Press, 2007], Ch. 1: '*Bildung* in Palestine: Bi-Nationalism and the Strains of German-Jewish Humanism') as follows:

'This was a nationalism that was guided essentially by inner cultural standards and conceptions of morality rather than considerations of power and singular group interest. Its exponents were united – as many saw it, in hopelessly naïve fashion – by their opposition to Herzl's brand of "political Zionism" both because they had distaste for his strategy of alliances with external and imperial powers and because they did not hold the political realm of Statehood to be an ultimate value: their main goal was the spiritual and human revival of Judaism and the creation of a moral community or common-wealth in which this mission could be authentically realized. To be sure, it is not always easy to sepa-rate the more general German and "cosmopolitan" ingredients from the recovered, specifically Jewish and religious dimensions of their vision.'

33 Ibid., 241.
34 Chaim Gans, *A Just Zionism: On the Morality of the Jewish State* (Oxford: Oxford University Press, 2008).
35 Walter Benjamin, 'Theses on the Philosophy of History', in *Illuminations*, trans. Harry Zohn (New York: Schocken, 1968), VI and XIV.

Chapter 10 Our Contemporary Heine: 'There are No Longer Nations in Europe'

1 Lecture delivered on receiving the Heinrich Heine Prize of the City of Düsseldorf on 14 December 2012.
2 Heinrich Heine, *Journey from Munich to Genoa*, in *The Works of Heinrich Heine*, translated from the German by Charles Godfrey Leland, Vol. 3 (London: William Heinemann, 1906), 103 (trans-lation amended). Citations in the text are from

the six-volume German edition of Heine's works, *Heinrich Heine: Sämtliche Schriften* (Munich: Hanser, 1969–76), edited by Klaus Briegleb.

3 Heine, *Ludwig Börne: A Memorial*, trans. Jeffrey L. Sammons (Rochester, NY: Camden House, 2006), 75.

4 Heine, *The Works of Heinrich Heine*, Vol. 8, 13 (translation amended).

5 Heine, *Religion and Philosophy in Germany*, trans. John Snodgrass (Albany, NY: SUNY Press), 51.

6 Heine, *Journey from Munich to Genoa*, 104.

7 Heine, *Religion and Philosophy in Germany*, 96.

8 Ibid., 121.

9 Ibid., 79.

10 Gerhard Höhn, *Heine-Handbuch*, Stuttgart: Metzler 1987, XI, 2. Aufl. 1997, VII.

11 Wolfgang Hädecke begins his biography (*Heinrich Heine* [Munich: Hanser, 1985]) with a summary of Heine's infamous memoirs, whose self-observations are not devalued by his tactical reasons for writing that work.

12 See ch. 12 of Jan-Christoph Hauschild and Michael Werner, *Heinrich Heine* (Cologne: Kiepenheuer & Witsch, 1997).

13 Karl Marx, *Critique of Hegel's Philosophy of Right* [1844], ed. and trans. Joseph O'Malley (Cambridge: Cambridge University Press, 1977), 132.

14 Heine, *Ludwig Börne: A Memorial*, 121.

15 Heine, *Lutetia*, Preface to the French Version, in Heine, *The Works of Heinrich Heine*, Vol. 8, 10.

16 Heine, *The Memoirs of Heinrich Heine and Some Newly-discovered Fragments of His Writings*, with an introductory essay by Thomas W. Evans (London: George Bell and Sons, 1884), 112.

17 Heine, *Heinrich Heine's Memoirs*, in two vols, ed. Gustav Karpeles, trans. Gilbert Cannan (London: William Heinemann, 1910), vol. 2, 249.

18 Heine, *Religion and Philosophy in Germany*, 153.
19 Quoted from Philip Kossoff, *Valiant Heart: A Biography of Heinrich Heine* (Cranbury, NJ, and London: Cornwall Books, 1983), 188–9.
20 Quoted from Anthony Phelan, *Reading Heinrich Heine* (Cambridge: Cambridge University Press, 2010), 231.
21 Heine, *Heinrich Heine's Memoirs*, 227.
22 Heine, *Confessions*, in Heine, *The Prose Writings of Heinrich Heine*, edited, with an introduction, by Havelock Ellis (London: The Walter Scott Publishing Company, 1887), 302 (translation amended).
23 Ibid., 312.
24 Ibid., 316.
25 Ibid., 307 (translation amended).